10 Secrets of Time Management for Salespeople

Gain the Competitive Edge and Make Every Second Count

By

Dave Kahle

CAREER
PRESS
Franklin Lakes, NJ

10 Secrets of Time Management for Salespeople
Edited by Nicole DeFelice
Typeset by Eileen Dow Munson
Cover design by Johnson Design
Printed in the U.S.A. by Book-mart Press

To order this title, please call toll-free 1-800-CAREER-1 (NJ and Canada: 201-848-0310) to order using VISA or MasterCard, or for further information on books from Career Press.

 CAREER PRESS

The Career Press, Inc., 3 Tice Road, PO Box 687,
Franklin Lakes, NJ 07417
www.careerpress.com

Library of Congress Cataloging-in-Publication Data

Kahle, Dave J.
    10 secrets of time management for salespeople : gain the competitive edge and make every second count / by Dave Kahle.
        p. cm.
    Includes index.
        ISBN 1-56414-630-8 (pbk.)
        1. Selling. 2. Time management. I. Title: Ten secrets of time management for salespeople. II. Title.

HF5438.8.T54 K34 2003
658.85—dc21

2002073350

Contents

Introduction:

It's a Daily Battle!

Remember the television commercial of the salesperson driving down the expressway with a cell phone balanced on his shoulder, a cup of coffee in one hand, and a laptop computer teetering on the dashboard? The voice in the background says, "You know he's out there."

That's a frightening commercial because of the element of truth in it. The life of a salesperson these days is a battle with an overwhelming number of things to do, ever rising expectations, and conflicting pressures.

While this has always been the case for field salespeople, in recent years the pressures have increased dramatically on every aspect of the salesperson's job. Customers are more sophisticated, more demanding, and harder to see. Voice mail has compounded the difficulty of the salesperson's job, making it necessary to be constantly on the phone. Whereas a few years ago a salesperson could visit a customer without an appointment, getting that appointment today adds multiple phone calls to the salesperson's job. Each phone call is one more task and one more small investment of time in an already full day.

The products and services offered by many salespeople have expanded in quantity and sophistication. As companies strive to meet the fracturing demands of their customers, the number of items sold has increased proportionately. I just finished a phone call with a sales manager who described a typical situation. His company, previously a software publisher with one basic product, had recently purchased a competitor. The combined sales force now has 11 products to sell. Every time a new product or service is introduced, it must be learned, the information must be filed, the presentation organized, etc. All of these things take time out of the salesperson's day. A salesperson with 10 things to sell must spend much more time dealing with information and organization than one with half as many offerings.

So, not only are customers' demands and the increasing number of products and services adding more pressure to the salesperson, but also the companies for whom they work are chipping in with additional demands. Salespeople are being asked to collect more information about their customers, report in more sophisticated ways, use more complex computer programs, and take part in more meetings than ever before.

The concept of the field salesperson as part of a "team" is growing more common. All that communication with team members adds more tasks to the salesperson's already long list. Each new task is an additional investment of time.

No wonder typical field salespeople feel like the weight of the world is pressing down on them. Their jobs have become overwhelming. Field salespeople are working more hours and as a result, feeling more stressed. Personal relationships fracture as spouses, children, and significant others are neglected. Production suffers as salespeople are confronted with too much to do and not enough time in which to do it.

At the same time, traditional time management guidelines have little application for the field salesperson. A few years ago, I watched a time management guru present a two-day seminar at an annual sales meeting for the company for which I worked. This university professor conveyed principle after principle of time management—all very appropriate if you worked in an office all day long, but very inappropriate if you were a field salesperson. The audience of field salespeople became more and more frustrated as the seminar progressed. Finally, one of my colleagues stood up and said, "You don't understand. We don't get interruptions, we are the interrupters!"

Clearly, most of the time management principles and tactics presented by this and other gurus totally miss the unique challenges of the field salesperson.

All of this may be moot if it doesn't impact you. So, before you read any further, reflect on whether you personally feel the weight of any of these pressures. Complete the assessment below:

1. Has the quantity of the products or services you sell increased in the last few years?

2. Have those products or services become more complex and sophisticated?

3. Are your customers more difficult to see today than they were three years ago?

4. Does voice mail give you fits?

5. Do your customers expect you to set appointments rather than just stop in?

6. Are customers more pressed for time when you see them?

7. Does your company require you to collect more information today than it did a few years ago?

8. Are you expected to complete more forms and attend more meetings, either in person or electronically, than previously?

9. Are you expected to work more closely with others in your organization, perhaps even be part of a team?

10. Do you find yourself working longer and harder than you did a few years ago?

11. Are your personal relationships suffering as a result of your stress and hours on the job?

12. Are you worrying about your personal performance?

A yes answer to any one of these is reason enough to focus on improving your time management skills. If you answered "yes" more than three times, you are ripe to crash and burn. Drop everything and read the rest of this book now!

Benefits of smart time management

Imagine that you have waved a magic wand and transformed yourself into a time management expert. You are now totally in control of your days, working at the most effective things, delegating wisely, and calmly producing excellent results. What would that mean to you?

How about your personal life? Wouldn't you have more time for the things you enjoy? Your spouse, kids, or friends would see you more often, and you would be less preoccupied with all the work stuff that fills your head. You'd get your life back!

Not only that, but you'd probably be healthier. You'd sleep better, your blood pressure would be lower, and you'd be and less anxious. It could add years to your life.

But what about your career? What would be the impact on your production?

As a veteran sales trainer, I can honestly report that improving your management of time will bring you positive results more quickly than any other single aspect of your job. That is because effective time management *frees* you. That's right, *frees* you. You unburden yourself of the countless petty tasks that fill your day. You cast off the shackles of the stuff you have to do, and instead, luxuriate in doing those things that you are good at, that give you joy, and that bring you the best results.

A number of years ago, I was impressed with the book *Soar With Your Strengths* by Donald Clifton and Paula Nelson. The premise of the book is that you are always more effective if you unleash your strengths than if you focus on overcoming your weaknesses. This is particularly true of salespeople, who have the ability to determine, to a large degree, how they spend their days.

Effective time management allows you to eliminate those things you must do that wear you down, sap your spirit, and weary your psyche—those weakness-generated tasks. Instead, you exercise your strengths, having become *free* of the burden of unpleasant minutia! And that always brings you more passion and better results.

The benefit of all of this is increased results, and more joy and fulfillment in your job and your life.

Obstacles in the way

If effective time management is such a powerful tool, why don't all salespeople naturally focus on it? Why do we struggle with it so much?

First, it's important to note that the really good salespeople are effective time managers. A few years ago, the National Society of Sales Training Executives published the results of a major research study. The study attempted to identify the characteristics of the superstar salespeople, across a variety of industries and products. They discovered that the nation's best salespeople had a number of characteristics in common. One was that they were "obsessed with time management." That was in the 1990s before today's heavy onslaught of "stuff to do" attacked the field salesperson. Imagine how much more of an impact effective time management has today.

So why is this such a big issue? Why aren't salespeople natural time managers?

The workday of the field salesperson, by its very nature, is unpredictable and constantly changing. It is not like you go to an office every day and methodically chip away at whatever is in your inbox. One day you may be working on one side of town, and the next on the other side of town. You may be calling on production supervisors in noisy manufacturing companies in the morning, and suit-and-tie CEOs in the afternoon. You may start out with five solid appointments, and have the first one call in sick, and the second be too busy to see you. Your most meticulous plans can be wiped out by an urgent call from a customer. Every day is an adventure for a field salesperson, often brimming over with the unpredictable ebb and flow of communications with dozens of people intensely pursuing their own agendas.

While, on one hand, most salespeople find this unpredictable kaleidoscope exhilarating, on the other, it's a major problem that presents unique challenges for managing time.

Here's another unique complication. Field salespeople, to a degree greater than almost any other job, are responsible for how they spend their time. Managers typically work in an office, where there is some accountability for their time. If their boss isn't around, their employees are, and they know what that manager has done all day. Goof off half the day and someone knows. This is true for the vast majority of jobs. Service people fill out meticulous job orders detailing how and where their time was spent. Inside salespeople, customer service people, purchasing agents, warehouse personnel, production people, are all accountable for their time, and to some degree, someone else dictates how their time will be spent.

This is not true for most field salespeople. You can probably take an afternoon off once a week, and it will be some time before anyone catches up with you. For the most part, you are the one who decides where to go, who to see, and when to do it. It's your decision to spend a half-day in the office every week, to do your paperwork at night, or to visit your good customers every other week.

Again, this independence is one of the aspects of the job that most field salespeople highly treasure. It's a powerful attraction for a lot of people. However, it brings with it enormous responsibilities. If you are independent and able to make your own choices about how you spend your time, then you must be more disciplined and attentive to time management than people who work in other jobs.

Here's another major obstacle unique to field salespeople: ourselves! The typical field salesperson has a personality that is inclined toward action. We like to be active, we like to be out and about, driving here, going there, and having 10 balls in the air at the same time. We find the rush of one thing after another to be exhilarating. We thrive on action.

Not everyone has that personality characteristic. But field salespeople generally do. That means that given the choice, we would rather get into our car and go someplace than sit in the office and think about it. That inclination towards activity is an obstacle. It causes us to go without necessarily thinking about why or where to go. It means we have to develop special disciplines and routines in order to hold our impulses in check, to make sure that they are applied in the most effective way.

One more final obstacle for field salespeople: the customer. I've often said that sales would be a really great job if it weren't for the customers. The problem is that salespeople need to be responsive to their customers. You can have the greatest plans for the day, but if a customer calls with a crisis, you need to stop everything and take care of the crisis. Customers are unpredictable. They make decisions when you don't think they will, they take longer to make up their minds than you expect, they want answers to questions you haven't even thought about, and they expect you to be available when you have other things to do. No matter how proactive and well planned you may be, your customers' requests are always the unknown, unpredictable X factor.

Let's pull all this together. Why is time management such a challenge for salespeople? Because of:

- The unique, ever-changing characteristics of the salesperson's day.

- A typical personality inclination toward activity.

- The unpredictable requests of the customers.

Introduction to the 10 secrets

I recall the moment when I first realized the importance of time management for salespeople. I was in my first professional sales position, and was making a lot of discoveries about how to be a good salesperson. As I was driving east on Interstate 96 between Grand Rapids and Lansing, Michigan, I had a sudden flash of inspiration:

**How you think about your job
when you are away from the customer is
just as important to your success as
what you say and do when you are
with the customer!**

All the decisions you make when you are not in front of the customer have a crucial impact on your success. Should you go here or there today? Should you do this in the office or at home? Should you call this customer or that one? Should you ask this question or some different one? Should you present this product or that one? Is this customer worth another phone call, or should you move on to find a new prospect?

These decisions, and countless others of a similar nature, determine your success as a salesperson. Of course, what you say and do when you are in conversation with a customer is important. But equally important are the decisions you make when you are by yourself.

One salesperson I know reflected that "Sales is a thinking person's game." How very true. The best salespeople know how to think about their jobs. It's the quantity and quality of thought that makes the difference. And good time management is 90-percent composed of thoughts about your job—it's the decisions you make when you are by yourself.

I have spent much of my professional career equipping people to "think about it."

My first book, written for distributor salespeople (*How to Excel at Distributor Sales*), was woven around the theme of thinking about your job. On the cover of my second book, *The Six-Hat Salesperson,* the publicist wrote, *"[the book] gives you a unique system that looks at all the pressures and challenges that you face, and shows you how to use **critical thinking skills** to make the most of every situation...."*

The 10 management secrets of good sales time management are, at their core, instructions on how to think about your job in such a way as to make the most effective use of your time.

The secrets have bubbled up through my own 30-plus years of field sales experience and been enhanced and further refined through the seminars I've done and my interaction with thousands of salespeople I've trained and helped develop. The secrets have taken shape over the years and been tested in the lives of salespeople around the world.

It is my belief, formed by years of observation and experience in working with tens of thousands of salespeople, that these management secrets have the power to transform your results, to allow you to sell more with less hassle, and to gain back fulfillment, joy, and leisure in your personal life.

In addition to the ten management secrets, you'll find a number of *"Tips From the Troops"* scattered throughout the book. These are specific time management tips that I've picked up along the way. Most have come from salespeople who have shared them at my seminars or sent them in to my monthly electronic newsletter. They are offered to you as an extra gift, compliments of all the salespeople who submitted them.

Enjoy!

The First Time Management Secret:

Get Grounded!

I've seen literally dozens of salespeople become superstars—record-setting prize winners who win the trips, earn the big commissions, and glow in the praises of the boss at annual sales meetings. And I've watched a considerable number of them crash and burn shortly thereafter.

Those who go down in flames follow some common patterns. Some compromise their integrity for the sake of the next big deal, and then pay the price of not being trusted by either their companies or their customers. Some abuse substances as they ride in the fast lane. Others become infatuated with their own success and squander their potential by chasing after some big deal that never closes. Most become immersed in the heady exhilaration of one deal after the other, work 12- to 14-hour days, and lose their families in the process.

Then there are those who excel and lead the pack year after year, who enjoy a full personal life, and view their success through a balanced perspective. The difference is that one group is grounded, and the other not.

What does it mean to be grounded? Being grounded means that you are securely fastened to some deeply held, basic commitments that give shape and focus to all that you do as a salesperson. Being grounded means that there is something that keeps you in check, that gives direction and purpose to your job-related efforts.

Imagine a kite flying in a brisk and variable wind. The kite twists and turns and darts up and down in response to the tricky winds. But it's always held in place by that string in the hands of its flyer, whose feet are firmly on the ground.

Cut that string, and the kite wiggles erratically and crashes to the ground. In a paradox, it's the string to the ground, that force that the kite constantly struggles against, that gives it the ability to fly. Cut the string, and the suddenly free kite instantly darts out of control and crashes to the ground.

So it is with grounded salespeople. Before you can concentrate on twisting and turning in response to the constantly changing winds of your job, you need to know that the string is firmly attached to the ground. Without it, you'll likely find yourself going off on tangents, becoming excessively reactive, and wasting hours every month in non-productive, low-priority efforts. That firm attachment is a strong commitment to something that is larger and longer-lasting than any individual part of your job. It's a paradox. In order to become more effective in your job, you must first focus on things that are outside of it.

Tips from the troops...

Make a duplicate set of essential items such as keys, your list of your credit card numbers, and a photocopy of your personal directory. That way, if any of this is lost or stolen, you won't waste time trying to recreate it.

When you *get grounded* you put that kite string in place, allowing you to focus on becoming effective in your job. Without being grounded, much of your effort to become more effective is scattered and unfocused.

There are three strands to this kite string, three elements to being grounded:

1. A mindset that provides energy for your efforts.

2. A basic strategy that gives direction to your efforts.

3. A set of important values that brings purpose to your efforts.

A mindset that provides energy for your efforts

Smart time management does not begin with the tools and tactics of your job. You don't start with a new PDA, laptop, or cell phone. Rather, you start inside yourself, by accentuating a mindset. A mindset is a group of beliefs that are so deep and firmly held that they are the source of many of your thoughts. Those thoughts kindle your behavior, influencing almost everything that you do. Your mindset shapes the way you see the world, and therefore, the way you do your job.

All the great time managers I have known have one thing in common. They have all shared the mindset that I call *More*. They believe that there is *more* to life than just this. There is *more* that you can do, *more* that you can become. There is *more* to your job than where you are at today. There is *more* challenge, *more* to achieve. There are *more* customers, *more* sales, *more* of everything.

They strive to do *more*, be *more* and have *more* because they believe that they can and they should. This fundamental mindset is a characteristic of every great achiever, whether they be a salesperson or a social worker, a politician or a preacher, a mother or a martyr.

Don't get this mindset mixed up with greed, which focuses on the accumulation of more and more money. The *More* mindset is not so trivial. It is focused on attaining a greater degree of human potential. Because of the salesperson's job, one portion of that human potential is measured by money. But that money is incidental to the drive for *more*. Some high achieving salespeople are salaried, compensated in such a way that their sales achievements do not directly impact their income. Some are still high achieving, *more* motivated people.

The *More* mindset concerns itself with not only doing *more* and having *more,* but also in becoming *more* than you are now.

When you are imbued with the *More* mindset, you never settle with the status quo. You know you can be better than you are, and you can achieve *more* than you do.

While we are considering *more* in relation to our jobs as salespeople, it has application to every part of our life. It's an approach to life.

More provides the energy that drives the changes you will need to make if you want to become an excellent time manager, because the *More* mindset creates discontent, and discontent is the mother of change.

Let's think about this together. If you are going to become a smart time manager, you are going to need to change some things that you do. Change is hard. None of us really likes to change. We'd much rather stay in our comfortable routines. We've spent years developing them, either consciously or subconsciously. If everything else were equal, we wouldn't change.

This is particularly true if we are solidly content with our situation and with ourselves. Show me salespeople who are perfectly content with who they are and what they are accomplishing, and I'll show you salespoeple who won't grow or improve.

Contentment, then, supports the status quo. Discontent is necessary to energize change. Take that same salesperson who is making a comfortable living and cause some change in those circumstances—cut the territory in half, or change the compensation plan. Or witness a personal change in circumstances—another child on the way, or the purchase of an expensive new home. Suddenly, there is discontent. That discontent causes energy, and energy, focused and directed in the right ways, causes positive change.

I'm not advocating that you go to your manager and ask for a cut in sales territory. But I am advocating that you understand the role of discontent in your job and the necessity to create discontent within yourself in order to energize the changes you'll need to make. I am advocating that you accept responsibility for developing your own discontent. And the way to create discontent in you is to latch on to the mindset of *More*.

If you truly believe that you can become better, do *more* and have *more*, then you are never content with the status quo. The *More* mindset becomes the seed that grows into constant discontent. The fruit of that tree is positive change.

Once you gain this *More* mindset, you find yourself engaging in certain kinds of behavior and developing certain habits. For example, because you believe that you can accomplish *more*, you look for opportunities to do so. You are more sensitive to opportunities for your products and services with your customers. The salesperson energized by the *More* mindset will find opportunities for products that the content salesperson will walk right by.

It works like this: The *More* mindset creates an expectation that there are *more* opportunities. Because you believe there are *more* opportunities, you look for them. Because you look for them, you find them. After a while, you begin to crystallize the processes and techniques you used to find those opportunities. You may create certain disciplines for yourself, like always asking an extra question or two. You may create tools, like an account profile form to capture customer opportunities. As a result, you become far more effective.

The starting point was the mindset. The mindset led to behavior. The behavior led to processes and habits. Those processes and habits led to better results.

Want to become a more effective time manager? Want to improve your sales results? Start with the first strand of the kite string—the *More* mindset.

How do you get the *More* mindset?

Many professional salespeople don't need to develop the *More* mindset. They already have it. It was instilled in them by their families as they were growing up. Part of their motivation to take a job in field sales in the first place may have come from that *more* mindset. There is, after all, *more* opportunity to do *more*, achieve *more*, become *more,* and have *more* in field sales then there is in most other jobs. The freedom of an outside salesperson leads to great opportunities for personal growth and financial achievement.

Looking back, I'd have to conclude that *more* was deeply instilled in me as I was growing up. My father was a salesperson who became a branch manager before he passed away. My mother, in her late 60s, became active in politics and was elected to three terms as city councilwoman in Toledo, Ohio. In her 70s, she was elected Vice Mayor of the city. Every one of my five brothers is self-employed. Clearly, some values were instilled in my family during my formative years.

If you have the *More* mindset as a result of your upbringing, be thankful. It was a wonderful gift to you from your family. It's a gift that will bring you a great share of abundance and affluence over the course of your life.

Another source of the *More* mindset is a firmly held spiritual belief. Spiritual beliefs are so deep inside us that they have the power to shape and direct our thoughts, our mindsets, our attitudes and, of course, our actions.

I happen to be Christian. I came to that position as an adult, at a time when I was searching for some meaning in my

Tips from the troops...

Before you meet, fax your agenda. That way your customer is prepared for the conversation you'll have with him or her.

life. I came to it as a result of a pretty thorough study of spiritual issues and religious paths. As a result, I have a deep-seated belief that God instilled certain gifts and talents in me, and that part of my appropriate response is to consciously exercise those gifts and talents in a way that strives for a more complete and influential use of them. In other words, *more*!

So, regardless of my upbringing, my deeply held spiritual beliefs have moved me to the *More* mindset.

Perhaps that is your story. If so, again be thankful that you have acquired the *More* mindset. It will lead to a richer and fuller life for you and those around you.

It may be, however, that you don't have *More* Mindset (M2) to any great degree. You vaguely sense that you can probably do better than you are, but it's not anything that you think much about. Or it may be that your *more* measure is temporarily down at the moment. You are going through a time of self-doubt. Your confidence is down, your self-image is suffering, and you are wondering if you are ever going to be more successful at this job.

Regardless of which of these two situations best describes you, the solution is the same. You need to replenish your *more* mindset. You need to reinvigorate your capacity to strive for more.

I have found that the best way to do so is to take charge of your thoughts by controlling the quality of material that goes into your mind. Instead of listening to talk radio or the latest "you left me sad and blue" country station, listen to a motivational or educational CD or cassette in the car. Instead of checking out every e-mail solicitation, subscribe to inspirational and educational e-newsletters (like mine!). Instead of hanging around with people who are complainers and fault-finders, surround yourself with upbeat, successful people. Instead of reading the latest psycho-mystery novel, read biographies of successful people (or buy my books!).

All of these are conscious choices you make that directly impact your thoughts, and your thoughts are the components of your mindset.

Want to improve your mindset? Want to increase your *more* measure? Take charge of the material that goes into your mind and watch your mindset shift.

Time management begins with a *more* mindset. You will never be a truly effective time manager without it. Make a decision right now to feed your *More* mindset.

The *More* mindset provides the first strand in our kite string—the energy to change in positive ways, for the rest of your life.

The next strand in your braided kite string provides the basic overall strategy that you will pursue in your quest for more.

More Mindset:
A set of deep-seated beliefs that you can and should have more, accomplish more, and be more than you are now.

The basic time management strategy

A house painter was determined to be the best, most profitable house painter in town. So he invested in the latest spray equipment, bought the quickest snap-together scaffolding and ladders, and trained at the gym to strengthen the muscles he needed to paint quickly. Using all these techniques, he painted his first house in 27 hours, when all of his competitors would have taken 40 hours to do the same job. As he sat in his truck and admired his work, he looked again at his job order and realized that he had painted the wrong house! He was incredibly *efficient*, and not at all *effective*.

> *Effective:* Doing the right things—those things that will get you the best results.
>
> *Efficient:* Doing things in a minimum amount of time.

This is one of the most common time management misconceptions resident in salespeople. Often, they focus too much on becoming efficient instead of effective; busying themselves with 1,000 tasks in the course of the day, but rarely stopping to ask if these are the right tasks. They'll buy a cell phone so that they can make phone calls from their car between sales calls. But they don't stop to consider whether those calls are worth making in the first place.

I can't emphasize this issue strongly enough. Gather 100 field salespeople together and ask them for a definition of time management, and 80 of them will talk about doing more in less time. While a little bit of that is appropriate, that is not the path to greater success in your job, less stress, and more enjoyment of your personal life.

Salespeople who view time management as the process of jamming more tasks into a day find themselves exhausted, highly stressed, burned out, and wondering why they don't accomplish more when they are working so hard. They become cynical, their blood pressure rises, they get irritable, and no one can stand to be around them. Not a pretty picture.

The way to the benefits that you want from smart time management is to follow the road called *effective*, not *efficient*. It is not doing more in less time; it is doing the best things with the time you have.

You can make great strides in time management and quantum leaps forward in your productivity by focusing on that which is effective, instead of just what is efficient. That means learning to prioritize that which will bring the greatest results from the smallest effort, not doing more in less time.

This focus on becoming more effective is the basic time management strategy for field salespeople. You'll find it cropping up over and over again throughout this book. If you are going to make the kind of progress that you hope to, then you must understand and commit to this basic strategy.

That's the second strand in our kite string.

The third strand provides the limits to your behavior, helping you to focus precisely.

Crystallizing your values

Imagine the *More* mindset as the engine that provides energy for your quest for better time management. Image the effective vs. efficient strategy as the basic path toward the attainment of the benefits you want. The final piece of the puzzle, the third strand of your kite string, is a set of values that hold you in check. Clear values provide boundaries around your journey so that you don't lose yourself in the rush to achieve your goals.

Whereas your mindset empowers you to move, values define the area in which you can and cannot operate.

Why is that important? It's a time saver. Think hard about the limits to your behavior. Spend a lot of time, crystallize them, write them down, and commit yourself to them. Then you don't have to think about them again. You'll be able to make thousands of decisions quickly and simply.

Let me illustrate. We have created a values statement for my business.

Values

Profit: We will earn a better-than-average profit as this allows us the flexibility to do other things.

Integrity: We will be honest in everything we do, never over promise, and zealously work to fulfill our commitments.

Value: We will strive to provide our clients more value than they expect.

Personable: We will be pleasant and easy to work with.

Knowledgeable: Understanding that we are in the business of "selling knowledge," we will be on the cutting edge of new knowledge.

Open-minded: We will constantly be open to new or different ideas, methods, and concepts from all sources, especially our clients.

Learning: We will value individual and organizational learning (the ability to continually take in new information, acquire new insights, and change in positive ways as a result of that information) as our primary competitive advantage.

Humility: We will constantly be aware that the resources we use and the clients we serve are gifts from God, entrusted to our temporary stewardship.

Quality: In everything we do, we will strive to do it as well as the very best companies in the world like ours do it.

Every employee receives a copy, we have copies prominently displayed around the office, and we expect everyone to be guided by these values. Having thought about them once, we don't need to reexamine every decision. The decisions come easily. Should we copy a piece of software we bought for this computer onto that one? No, it would be dishonest. Should we send out this letter without proofreading it three times? No, it would mean lower quality. Should we invest in this seminar? Yes, it provides us with new ideas, one of our values. Got the idea?

When you write out a set of values for your sales life, you shape and focus your behavior, making it easy to make decisions. Values, clarified and articulated, are a great time saver.

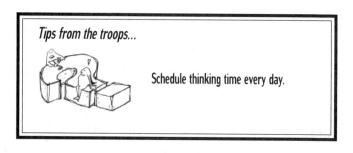

Tips from the troops...

Schedule thinking time every day.

We all have values. Those are the things, people, institutions, habits, and behaviors we think are more important than others. Sometimes we are aware of these values, and make conscious, intelligent decisions to value something or someone. That's the decision you made, for example, if you are married. You consciously chose to highly value the person who became your spouse.

More commonly, we are not aware of all the things we value. We haven't chosen them thoughtfully. So, we value things, but we have not really examined them, to ascertain whether they are worthy of our time and effort. We just inherited them, picking them up from our families in our early years. As adults, however, we have an opportunity to examine our values, and to choose those that are higher and more noble than others. It's not enough to be consistent and true to your values, but you must also chose higher values. Hitler, for example, was true to his values. He pursued his vision and was, for a time, successful in it. But his was not a noble value.

Start with a list

It's the dreaded blank piece of paper. You are going to fill it with answers to different questions. Work through them methodically.

1. *What people do you value?*

2. *What ideas or movements are important to you?*

3. *What behaviors do you respect?*

4. *What character qualities do you admire?*

5. *What irritates you about other people or situations?* Those things that bother you are usually the absence of something you value. For example, if a rude person irritates you, it's because you value politeness.

This is just a start. The idea is to create a long list of the things that you determine to be more important than any one deal, any one small accomplishment. For example, by publishing my company's value statement, I am taking the position that these values are more important than any single transaction, more important than money or accomplishment. If there is some financial gain to be had, for example, by being dishonest, we won't do it. Why? Because our value of honesty is more important than any deal.

That's the real issue. What values are most important to you? What attitudes, behaviors, people, or ideas will you sacrifice other things for? Write those down, creating a long list.

Edit

Just like with other aspects of your job, too long a list diffuses your energy and causes more of a problem than is solves. Remember: focus, focus, focus. When you have a long list, look for patterns. Edit and prioritize your list, ferreting out the things that pop up over and over again. Work at it until you have a one-page document. Let it sit for a few days, then review it a few times. Is this really who you are? Are you willing to commit to these things? Are they worth sacrificing for?

When you are happy with the document, congratulate yourself because now you are done! You have put in place the three braided strands of your kite string. You've done the hard work of becoming grounded. Now, you are free to soar!

Don't just file your work away in that box that has last year's income tax return and your high school pictures. Share your work with people close to you. Post reminders in prominent places. Set your value statement up as a screensaver on your laptop. Put a *More* reminder in your calendar to review in order to refresh yourself annually. More importantly, keep it on your mind, and use it to direct your decisions and focus your energy.

Why bother?

Why should a busy salesperson take time to work on these "grounding" issues that may, at first, seem only indirectly related to time management? The kite string analogy is nice, but does it operate in real life? Here's how.

I. Writing out your values forces you to focus with some precision.

One of the overwhelming challenges of the information age is sorting through all the possibilities available to you. You will need to continually struggle with *focus.* The more you can focus on the important things in your life and your job, the more successful you will be. You'll shrug off the onslaught of trivial diversions, and keep your energies applied to the place where they will get the best response.

Reducing things to writing causes you to focus. This exercise means that you take those vague and general ideas that float around in your head, and think precisely, reducing them to words on paper. Words precisely written clarify the gray areas in which many of us spend a lot of our time.

2. A written statement commits you.

In every new employee orientation, we provide a written statement that describes my company's vision, values, and ethics. That statement also hangs on the wall in highly visible areas. The fact that it exists in writing is a commitment. Our employees know exactly what ethical behavior is expected of them. Because it is in writing, and posted prominently, they know I'll hold them accountable to that standard, and that they can hold me to it also.

If that statement were not written out, it would not have the same power. It's one thing to state something orally, but it's quite another to commit ourselves to a position in writing. Every important position in human affairs is written out and turned into a document of some kind. *The Declaration of Independence*, *The Constitution*, and the Bible are written documents.

I have occasionally been involved in organizations where there was an extremely manipulative person. On each of those occasions, the person in question strongly resisted written policies and procedures. The reason? If it was in writing, it was understood and agreed to. It represented some rules— limits on what the organization's members could and could not do. If it didn't exist in writing, then there was room to maneuver and to manipulate.

Those same principles apply to us. If we have some values and ethics, but we don't write them out, we've left ourselves wiggle room. We're not as committed as we should be. That wiggle room means that we can maneuver and rationalize if we want to. And that ultimately reduces our effectiveness and wastes our time.

3. A written statement provides you with guidance in making decisions.

The results of these exercises can simplify your life greatly and provide a powerful tool to help you focus. Think deeply about certain issues once, get them resolved, and then you don't have to think about them again. You may decide that you are going to be absolutely honest in all dealings with your customers and employers. Okay, you've made a decision, committed it to writing, and let some other people know about it. When that opportunity comes up to get a sale by allowing a customer to maintain an incorrect assumption, you don't have to think about. You don't have to take your time to consider it. You just don't do it. Simple. Easy. You don't need any time to think about that one.

Tips from the troops...

Call the person whose extension is one digit apart from the person you want to talk with. Often that gets you the person at the next desk. Ask them to put a message on the desk of the person you are trying to reach.

That's because you thought about it deeply once. Now, you don't have to go through that thought process again. You have created a standard to guide your decisions. That guide simplifies your decisions and allows you to make them quickly and confidently. You've saved time.

4. A written statement helps keep you from being overwhelmed.

When you have a mindset, a basic strategy, and a set of values and priorities, these help you sort through the over-whelming number of things to do, and choose wisely between them. Here's how it works.

Let's say that *More* mindset has caused you to commit to a certain long-term goal: to rise in the corporate ranks as high as you can go. So you've chosen to pursue a long-term career with your company and you want to move up the corporate ranks. It's toward the end of the month, and you are over-whelmed with stuff to do. You've got a number of projects you are trying to close, your boss wants you to get a certain number of new customers, you have some customer problems to take care of, there is some new training available from the corpo-rate office, etc. You can't possible do everything you need to do. Some things are not going to get done. Which ones? How do you sort it out?

You take your *more-generated* long-term goal, and rank each task in priority in light of the goal. You ask, Which of these tasks is going to move me closer to my goal? Then, make a list of all the things you have to do. Next, put the items in priority, from the most important to the least, understanding that those on the bottom of the list probably won't get done.

Now, plan to work at the most important things. Presto! Your long-term goals have helped you sort out your overwhelm-ing number of tasks and kept you from being overwhelmed.

5. A written statement provides motivation in times of adversity.

There have been a number of times in my career where things were not going very well—it seemed like I couldn't sell anything, I was not getting along with my boss, and my family life was falling apart. My performance problems on the job hurt my income, and that lack of money added stress to my personal life, which in turn caused me to be irritable with my boss and short with my customers. A vicious cycle.

At these times, it was only my sense of a larger purpose, of something bigger than myself, that allowed me to put the situation into perspective. As a result, I was able, at every one of these miserable times in my life, to work through them, to survive, and even prosper.

If there is one sure thing in the life of a salesperson, it is this: You will have to face some serious adversity sometime in the future. It may come from a work-related issue—a deep sales slump, a cut in compensation, a new boss who doesn't like you, or a serious change that impacts you negatively. Or it may come from a more personal source and impact your performance—problems with a spouse or family member, or perhaps health problems. Regardless, it will come. I guarantee it.

Your ability to successfully deal with it will be one of the watershed moments of your career. Allow it to depress you and you'll slide down that downward spiral, cheating yourself and your family of the fruits of success. Overcome it, and you'll strengthen your character and contribute to the lives of your family. It's one of the most important issues you'll face.

Michael Gelb put it well in his book *Thinking for a Change:*

The greatest long-term predictor of success for individuals and organizations is resilience in the face of adversity. Individuals and organizations who view their setbacks in the context of progress are much more likely to continue in their efforts toward success.

I couldn't agree more. When you have a larger purpose, clearly articulated, written out and committed to, then every difficulty and adversity is just another step toward that end. If you don't, then even the smallest obstacle can be seen as insurmountable.

6. A written statement provides motivation to stretch yourself.

It's very easy to get comfortable in a routine and never vary from that. Or to become complacent. It is probably a natural human motivation. We work hard to get to the point where we don't have to work hard anymore. The problem with that is that when we become complacent, we stop growing. We stop gaining new skills, expanding our capability, broadening and deepening our perspectives.

From time to time, we need to be stretched to take risks beyond the limits of our comfort. The *More* mindset, coupled with a basic strategy and a well-articulated set of values, provides us the motivation to go beyond what we have done in the past and to expand ourselves.

At one point in my career, I was the number-one salesperson in the nation for a company—my first full time professional sales job. I had it made—adequate salary, good benefits, company car, bonus potential, and the respect of my employer and my colleagues. But I became bored and decided to move on to a job that was 180 degrees different. I took a job selling surgical staplers to hospitals. It was a huge leap from the secure job I had to one that paid straight commission, in which I had to buy my own samples and literature from the company, and work totally on my own.

Because of some experiences in my childhood, I hated hospitals. I had never worked on straight commission before, never sold to doctors, and had absolutely no knowledge of surgical procedures. When I accepted that job, that was a stretch for me.

I was able to take that stretch and put myself into an uncomfortable place primarily because I had a more-generated vision of myself as a very competent, successful salesperson who was on his way to bigger things. It was because of my grounding in deeper issues that I was able to take this leap.

So it is with you. If you have the three kite strings in place, then you have the motivation to stretch yourself beyond your current limits.

Don't neglect these basic issues. If you want to become a smart time manager, first get grounded.

To implement this management secret:

1. Feed your *More* mindset with books, tapes, seminars, and positive people. Do something each week to strengthen your beliefs in *more*.

2. Make sure you understand the difference between effective and efficient. Think of an example, in your own words from your job, in which you did something to become more effective, and another in which you did something to become more efficient. Identify and solidify your values. Write them down, share them with people close to you, and post them in a prominent location. Remind yourself of them regularly.

3. Check my Website (*www.salestimemanagement.com*) for our Time Management Tool Kit. including forms and worksheets.

The Second Time Management Secret:

Think About It Before You Do It!

How many times have you gotten up in the morning and headed out for your first call without a clear idea of what you were going to do once you arrived there? Or how often have you arrived at a sales call and realized that you didn't have everything you needed for that call? Has your manager ever asked you for a monthly plan, and you didn't have any ready response?

All of these are indications of one of the field salesperson's most common tendencies: to act before you think. It's a frequently occurring malady from which even the best and most experienced salespeople suffer.

It is a symptom of a deeper condition—the inclination toward action, which is a personality trait typical of field salespeople. We like being active, we like confronting the world, solving problems, and making things happen. So we can go through a day, a week, a month, a year, even a career by bouncing from one problem to be solved to another.

Imagine a popcorn maker—the older style that consisted of a hot plate surrounded by a glass jar. Put the popcorn and some hot oil in the bottom, and turn the popcorn maker on. Pretty soon the oil will start to sizzle, and one of the kernels will explode and career up and against the side of the glass canister. A second or two later another will do the same. Before long, dozens of popcorn kernels are exploding with bursts of energy and bouncing around in a display of totally unfocused power.

Many salespeople are like that. A customer calls with a problem, Bam! Go fix it. Another calls and wants a quote on something. Pow! Chase after that. Before long, we're expending a tremendous amount of energy, responding and reacting to the slightest pull and tug of our customers. We're like that popcorn, exploding in countless directions. Just imagine what we could accomplish if we could harness all that power and focus it in one direction.

That's what this management secret is all about. Focus. Disciplining yourself to invest a certain quantity of time in order to focus your efforts where they will return the greatest amount to you. You do that by disciplining yourself.

Think About It Before You Do It!

Notice the word *discipline*. It's a key concept for smart time managers. What's a discipline? It's an exercise or a process to which you commit yourself. You repeatedly engage in it because you know it's a good thing to do. You know that it will bring you good results, even though it may not be that pleasant or exciting.

I discipline myself to swim laps a couple of mornings each week, for example. Honestly, I don't particularly enjoy getting up early, especially in the winter, and driving off in the cold and dark to jump into a swimming pool of cool water, and mindlessly laboring back and forth for 35 minutes. It's not high on my list of pleasurable activities. But I've done it regularly for almost 20 years. Why? Because I know that it is good for me. It prevents lower back pain, increases my energy, reduces stress, and enables me to put in a calm and focused day. It's a discipline.

A pilot preparing to fly an airliner first goes through a checklist of items. Most pilots have done that checklist hundreds or thousands of times. I'm sure they would rather be doing something else than sitting in the cockpit methodically working through a checklist of items to review. Why do they do it? It's a discipline that results in safer flights.

There are certain disciplines for salespeople that will bring about good results when they are practiced regularly. *Thinking about it before you do it* is one such discipline.

Remember my discussion of obstacles to effective time management in the first chapter? I talked about that inclination in the personality of most salespeople to act first and think later. I also discussed the rapid flow of events that often crowd into a salesperson's day, making immediate reaction too often the primary mode of dealing with things. Because of this potent combination of pressures—one internal and one external—it's important that salespeople build certain disciplines into their routines. These disciplines protect us from ourselves and allow us to handle the furious confluence of stuff we have to deal with.

This management secret requires that you spend a certain amount of time in the discipline of directed thought. In the next chapter, I'll discuss the *quality* of that time, but for now, our focus is the right *quantity*.

The planning cycle

Smart time managers discipline themselves to adhere to a cycle of planning events and processes. This cycle should become part of the discipline of every field salesperson. The cycle looks like this:

- ▣ An annual planning retreat of one to three days.

- ▣ Quarterly planning sessions of one-half to one day.

- ▣ Monthly planning sessions of approximately one-half day.

- ▣ Weekly plans.

- ▣ Daily preparation.

- ▣ Pre-call preparation.

- ▣ Post-call reflection.

Over the years, I've developed a guideline that works very well for field salespeople:

> **Spend approximately 20 percent of your time thinking about the other 80 percent.**

Now, that doesn't mean that you get to take every Friday off. But it does mean that you discipline yourself to invest sufficient time in planning and preparing so that your time will be more effectively used. It does mean that you follow this planning cycle.

Annual planning retreat

One of my clients brings all of his salespeople into the office for a planning retreat once a year. In this retreat, every salesperson creates sales goals for every category of product they sell and for every account they serve. This information is then entered into the computer, and becomes part of the standard by which that salesperson is measured.

Another client does something similar. Salespeople come together for an annual goal-setting and strategy-developing retreat. At this three-day event, they meet with their sales manager and create specific goals for the year. With the manager, they jointly develop the overall strategy for achieving those goals.

It is not unusual for a company to gather its salespeople together, bring me in to do a "sales time management" seminar, and then follow that with a couple days of intense planning.

You may be thinking, "Isn't this is lot of unnecessary paperwork? Aren't the salespeople wasting time being out of the field?" No, just the opposite. These companies have wisely created special planning times for their sales force because they know that it's worth the time and money that it takes.

It may be that your company organizes a similar planning event. If so, good for you. If not, then you need to organize it yourself. Remember, it is one of the disciplines of the most successful salespeople.

Find a time of year when you are the least busy. I find the time between Christmas and New Year's Day to be perfect for me, but you may have a different time. Block out one to three days in that time period, and don't schedule any appointments for those days.

Find a space where you can work virtually uninterrupted. This may take some creativity. I doubt if it's your company office. It may be your home if you have a room in which you can seal yourself off. One year, I was one of two people responsible for leading an organization. The two of us drove to a state park, climbed in the back of my old conversion van, and worked in the back of the van all day long. We were isolated and uninterrupted.

Gather the materials you'll need: all your account folders, account profiles, your company's goals for the year, information about key products, services, or categories, computer print-outs of last year's sales, maps of your geographical territory, and anything else you may want to review.

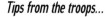

Tips from the troops...

When you are eating lunch in a restaurant, order immediately. Keep the waiter there when he brings the menu and make a quick decision.

Focus on what you are going to produce in this planning event—the output or result of your efforts. You are going to create these things:

- ▣ A set of sales goals for your territory.

- ▣ A basic strategy for reaching those goals.

- ▣ A well-defined ABC analysis of your customers and prospects.

- ▣ Individual goals and strategic plans for each of your key (A) accounts.

- ▣ A basic territory plan.

- ▣ A set of learning goals.

Sounds arduous, and it is. But when you spend disciplined, focused time thinking about these things in detail, it will allow you to do good work; to prepare the best, most effective plans that you are capable of; and it will free you to implement effectively when you are in the field.

Later in the year, you won't be tempted to head out on Monday morning without a clear plan in mind, because you have spent this time formulating the plan. And when the press of customer problems and inquiries threatens to overwhelm you and force you into becoming too reactive, you'll be held on track by the goals and plans you created in your planning discipline.

Outcomes

Let's consider three of these outcomes of your planning retreat.

1. A set of sales goals for your territory.

Your work should lead you to a series of sales goals for your territory. In order to get there, you must first determine the categories of goals that you are going to create. It may be that you work for a company that has already determined this, like my clients described above. If so, good for you. If not, then it will be up to you to determine your own set of categories. Depending on your unique set of products and services and your company's emphasis, you may create goals for the following, most frequently used, categories:

A. Total sales.

B. Total gross margin.

C. Number of units.

D. Total sales per product category (dollars, gross margin, or units) for each of several categories of product or service that you sell.

E. Goals for acquiring new accounts.

This is just a list of the most common sales goals. You can have a virtually unlimited variety of goals. The categories of goals are up to you, your company, and your manager.

I'd suggest no more than five categories. Remember, one of the reasons you create goals is to help you focus your energies on the most important issues, and thus become more effective. More than five goals defeats that purpose. Too many goals cause you to diffuse your energies, not focus them.

Tips from the troops...

Don't waste time with accounts that can't bring themselves to say NO. If you sense that they fit this category, ask them for a clear Yes or No. Sometimes forcing a "no" decision saves you months of wasted time.

Let's illustrate. Assume that I sell sophisticated cleaning equipment and supplies to three different market segments: manufacturers, school systems, and shopping malls. My product line consists of a series of heavy-duty floor cleaning machines and the associated supplies used by those machines. I select the following categories to create goals:

1. Total sales.

2. Total number of cleaning machines.

3. Total number of Superscrubbers, our new, high-tech machine.

4. Number of new accounts.

5. Total sales of supplies (as opposed to equipment).

Now that you have determined the categories on which to focus, you need to create specific numbers for each. This is where the art comes in. You consider your company's goals and your understanding of what the market is doing. You factor in your best understanding of what your competitors are doing, and you consider your customers' situations and yours. Out of this comes your best attempt to predict a result that will cause you to stretch, but not be unreasonable.

I prefer to look at each account individually, think about it, and determine it's likely contribution to each of the categories. Examine each account, analyze the potential, consider your situation, and determine a realistic goal. Go on to the next account, and do the same. Then compile each of the numbers from the specific accounts, and presto! You have an annual number.

Let's go through this process for a few accounts in our sample territory. As you begin your planning session, you have all your account folders filed alphabetically, so you begin with the first, AAA Industrial. This account is expanding its facility, and will need to add two machines. You may be able to get them to upgrade one or two of their older units at the same time. The competition isn't very active in this account, and you expect to get the equipment business as well as all the supplies that go along with it. That means three new machine sales of about $60,000, supplies of about $20,000 and no new Superscrubbers—this account is quite happy with the current technology.

On to the next account—Alalema Public Schools. Here, they are talking about replacing some of their older machines. But they have a new director of maintenance, whom you haven't met. Their supplies are awarded on an annual bid, and you don't have that business because the competition underbid you. You think it's going to take some work to get a new machine or two out of this account, so you add one machine at $20,000 to your list, no Superscrubbers, and no supplies. On to the next account.

And so it goes. You methodically review each account, think about it in detail, develop a realistic goal for each, and then compile those numbers for your annual goal.

Back to the example. Let's say we've done this, and come up with a set of annual goals that looks like this:

1. Total sales = $1,765,000.

2. Total number of cleaning machines = 62.

3. Total number of Superscrubbers = 16.

4. Number of new accounts = 10.

5. Total sales of supplies = $1,000,000.

You're still not finished. Now, you need to work those out on a quarterly or monthly basis. In our example, we've elected to use quarterly numbers. So, our final goal-setting exercise ends up looking like this:

Quarterly Sales Goals				
	1st	2nd	3rd	4th	Totals
Sales	$400,000	$475,000	$500,000	$390,000	$1,765,000
Machines	12	18	22	10	62
Super-scrubbers	2	4	6	4	16
New Accounts	2	3	3	2	10
Supplies	$200,000	$250,000	$325,000	$225,000	$1,000,000

2. A well-defined ABC analysis of your customers and prospects.

This is an issue we'll describe in detail in the next chapter.

3. Individual goals and strategic plans for each of your key (A) accounts.

If you are in the kind of selling position where you are attempting to sell more to certain key accounts, then you need to create specific, monthly strategic plans for each of those key accounts. When we consider the fourth management secret, we'll discuss in detail the concept of identifying your highest potential accounts and then investing more time in these "A" accounts and less time in the others. For now, let's assume that you have prioritized your accounts and that you have a list of your "A" accounts.

In the typical sales territory, around 50 to 80 percent of your business is going to come from this group of accounts. That means that these accounts warrant special attention, special preparation, and special thought. You ought to apply the disciplines we have already discussed to your "A" accounts. In other words, create annual sales goals for each "A" account, create annual strategic plans for each, review progress on each account in your quarterly reviews, and develop specific monthly plans for each "A" account.

Quarterly planning sessions

Once a quarter, discipline yourself to dedicate planning time in a mini-planning retreat. All the rules and guidelines from the annual retreat apply to this, only the duration under consideration is shorter and not nearly as intense. So, lock yourself up in some secluded place, and focus on the task at hand.

Your purpose is to revise and fine-tune the decisions and plans you made in the annual planning retreat. So you review each of your goals, and the progress you have made in each of your "A" accounts, and you refine and revise your plans.

Monthly planning sessions

Create a master plan every month. This is your basic operational document. In it, you consolidate all your plans, pull them together, and make them very specific. This document, two to three pages in length, contains your monthly goals, your key account goals, your learning plan, a basic strategic plan for how you are going to accomplish your goals, and a weekly territory plan. See the Tool Kit for examples of different formats for monthly plans.

Weekly plans

At the end of every week, take 30–60 minutes to organize the next week, to review where you are going, to fold in anything that didn't get done the previous week, and to gather the supplies, samples, and folders you'll need.

Daily plans

At the end of every business day, set aside 30 minutes or so to prepare for the next day. Put your plan together, and gather everything you need for the next day. By doing this at the end of the previous day instead of the morning of the next day, you clear your mind to enjoy the balance of the day with your family and friends, and you enable yourself to start off energetically in the morning.

Pre-call review

Spend a few minutes in the car before you go in to see your customer for every sales call. If you are working on the phone, take a moment or two to prepare yourself for the phone call. Ask yourself several questions:

- ▣ Why am I here?

- ▣ What value am I bringing the customer in this call?

- ▣ What do I want to accomplish?

- ▣ How am I going to do that?

- ▣ Do I have all the materials I'll need?

You may even want to close your eyes and see the sales call happen in your imagination. Imagine yourself talking, and your customer doing likewise. See the sales call successfully unfolding, like you were watching a movie. This technique, called imaging, plants ideas in your subconscious, and is a way to

Tips from the troops...

Work while you wait on the phone.

quickly and subtly "practice" a sales call. Get good at this thinking process and you'll see a major improvement in the quality of your sales calls.

Post-call reflection

I'm probably stretching this management secret a bit by including this particular thinking process. The management secret is *think about it before you do it,* and this process requires you to think about it *after* you do it. However, because the purpose of thinking about it *"after"* you do it is to make changes *before you do it again*, this post-call reflection fits.

One of the best times to make changes and improve your results is just after you've made a sales call. This is another discipline of the best salespeople. Set aside a few moments after your sales call, and think about it. Ask yourself several questions:

▣ What went well?

▣ What did I do to make that happen?

▣ What went poorly?

▣ What could I have done differently to get better results?

▣ What should I do differently next time?

Do this every day, and it won't be long before you'll begin to notice significant improvements in the quality of your sales calls.

Smart time managers understand the power of planning. They know that they are always more effective if they *think about it before they do it.* And they know that the discipline of regular planning time (20 percent of their average workweek) will bring results far in excess of the time spent planning.

To implement this management secret:

1. Right now, before you forget, open your planner or electronic calendar, and schedule the planning times discussed in the chapter.

   - An annual planning retreat of one to three days.

   - Quarterly planning sessions of one-half to one day.

   - Monthly planning sessions of approximately one-half day.

   - Weekly plans.

2. Every day for the next three weeks, focus on ending the day by planning and preparing for the next day. By then, it should have become a habit that you will do instinctively.

3. Do the same with pre- and post-call planning. Make a commitment right now to invest a few minutes before and after every call to thinking about it.

The Third Time Management Secret:

Think Right!

While it is important to *think about it before you do it*, and invest a sufficient *quantity* of time in thinking and planning, it is just as important to improve the *quality* of that time. To do that, you need not only to think about it, but you also need to think about it *in the right way*.

How you think has more impact on your performance than any other thing you do. In one sense, everything you do in time management is a result of a thinking process. This entire book is about thinking.

In this chapter, however, we're going to examine some very specific thinking processes, and equip you with an understanding of how to think in ways that will bring you the best results.

Thinking is like golf. Very few people are natural golfers who figure out the mechanics of the game all by themselves. You can practice hitting the ball every day at the driving range and try to learn by trial and error, or you can save a lot of time and effort and make great leaps forward in your golfing abilities by having a pro give you a few lessons. In golf, it's not just the quantity of practice; it's the quality.

So it is with thinking. You can think all you want, but if you don't do it the right way, it's a waste of your time. You can religiously discipline yourself to the quantity of thinking we discussed in Management Strategy Two, but if you don't do the right kind of thinking, you are wasting most of your time.

Just like there are processes for making a sales call and persuasively presenting your product or service, there are proven processes for thinking about it before you do it. Master these step-by-step thinking processes and you will improve the quality of your thinking. And that improvement in the quality of your thinking will lead to improvement in the results you get.

I'm certainly not the first person to make this observation.

*The one feature that all the most successful
organizations I have been concerned
with have shared is, quite simply, the ability to think
better than their rivals.*

—Ben Heirs, *The Decision Thinker*

As a man thinks in his heart, so is he.

—King Solomon

There is an age-old principle here. Your thoughts determine your actions. Your actions, repeated, build habits. Your habits, assembled, become your character. And your character determines the results you achieve in your life.

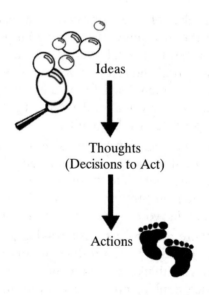

Ideas

Thoughts
(Decisions to Act)

Actions

So, it behooves you to think right. When you do, you can gain a tremendous advantage over your competitors, who haven't read this book.

Thinking processes for effective time management

There are a few thinking processes that are essential for you to master if you are going to be an effective time manager. They are:

- ▣ Analyzing.

- ▣ Planning.

- ▣ Prioritizing.

- ▣ Imaging.

- ▣ Reflecting.

Let's examine each of these thinking processes.

Analyzing

The dictionary definition of *analyzing* that most accurately describes our usage is: *to break into its component parts*. For all practical purposes, everything can be broken up into its component parts. That's easy to understand when we think of physical objects. Look up from reading this for a moment and look at some physical object around you. Maybe it's a chair across the room. Can you break that chair down into its component parts? Of course. There is the wooden structure, the foam padding, and the fabric upholstery.

Can we take it a level deeper and break one of those components, say the wooden structure, down into its component parts? Of course. There are the vertical braces, the wooden dowels, the glue that holds the pieces together, the screws that fasten things together, and the horizontal members.

Can we take that one layer deeper? Of course. Let's look at one of the vertical braces. There is varnish and stain on the surface of the wood, and within the piece itself, sections that can be labeled hard wood or soft wood. We can continue this process until we get to the point that the physicists argue about. But that's irrelevant to our purposes. On a day-to-day, practical level, everything we touch, see, or work with can be broken down into component parts.

What is true for physical objects around us is also true for the major parts of our jobs. We can break down our jobs into their component parts. Then, we can break each of those component parts into its respective parts, and so on.

But, you're thinking, what's the use? Why would I do that?

Because analyzing is a powerful, necessary thinking process if you are going to make effective use of your time. Because when you are overwhelmed with too much to do and not enough time in which to do it, you must make good decisions about what to do. Making good decisions about what to do means that you must think about it first. And thinking about it means that you must analyze it, break it down into its component parts, and select those parts that will bring you the best results. All superior salespeople are excellent analysts.

When you take your planning retreat, you are going to analyze your customers, prospects, and products.

Tips from the troops...

While you are with a customer, make an appointment then for the next visit, even if it is months away. This eliminates several voice mail messages and phone calls trying to make contact to create the appointment.

When you do your quarterly and monthly planning, you are going to analyze your strategy within each account.

When you do your weekly planning, you are going to analyze your strategy and your weekly goals.

Before and after each sales call, you are going to analyze the call and the customer. For example, you may have finished a sales call and not been happy with the results. You think to yourself, "That didn't go well." So you ask yourself, "What went wrong in that call?" In order to answer that question, you must break down the call into its component parts—you analyze it. You think, "At the beginning of the call, Bill seemed distracted. I wasn't able to help him feel comfortable with me. But I did a thorough job of describing our proposal. He asked some appropriate questions. But he wouldn't commit to any next step."

You've broken down the call into some of its component parts, and found a couple of suspects—your ability to make him feel comfortable with you and his unwillingness to commit. Your analysis has helped you determine where the problem was. Now, you're equipped to make some changes the next time.

As you can see, analyzing is a necessary, regular part of your job if you are going to be more effective.

So, let's take your job as a whole and break it down into its major component parts. What are the major parts of your job? Most field salespeople would respond to that question with a list that looks like this:

- Dealing with customers.

- Dealing with prospects.

- Interacting with internal personnel.

- Planning.

- Reporting and paperwork.

- Understanding your products and services.

At this point, you've analyzed, on a very superficial level, the major tasks you face. Now let's pick one of these components, and break down that one into its component parts. Let's pick your customers. How would you take this idea of "customers" and break it down into its component parts? This is where it becomes a bit more complicated. *We need to decide what criteria to use.* You could break them down by the criterion of *type*. For example, of the 100 customers you have, 20 are retailers, 35 are contractors, and 45 are OEM manufacturers.

Or you could choose to break them down using the criterion of *size*. Of those same 100 customers, 10 have less than 20 employees, 50 have between 21 and 50, 20 have between 51 and 75, and 20 have more than 76 employees.

When you analyze, you first select the thing to analyze, you then select the criterion, and then you break the thing apart using that criterion.

Here's an easy way of visualizing this. Image a big sledgehammer. When you swing that sledgehammer and hit something, the force breaks that thing into a bunch of little pieces. You have a rock in front of you. Swing the sledgehammer and bam! The rock has become 20 smaller pieces. You have a large ice block on the floor in front of you. Hit it with the sledgehammer and bam! Lots of little ice pieces.

The sledgehammer is an image to help you analyze. You take your mental tool—the sledgehammer—and hit the thing you are analyzing, breaking it into several smaller pieces. Each piece is a part of the original. Only now you use it on a mental object.

The sledgehammer is the criterion you use, and the act of swinging the sledgehammer is the actual process of applying that criterion to your object.

The easiest way to do this is to memorize and apply two questions. The answer to the first question forms the sledgehammer. That question is: "What criterion should I use?" Answer that, and you have the sledgehammer in your hands.

Now ask yourself the second question: "What are the key component parts of this?" When you do that, you swing the sledgehammer and smack the object you are analyzing.

Let's practice. Hit your "customers" with the sledgehammer, like we did above. We ask the question, "What criterion should I use." Answer: "Type of customer." Swing that hammer by asking, "What are the key component parts of this?"

"Customers" analyzed by type
- *20 retailers*
- *35 contractors*
- *45 OEM manufacturers*

Let's take the object, "Everything you have to do tomorrow," and hit it with the sledgehammer. Ask the question, "What criterion should I use?" Answer, "business tasks." Swing the hammer by asking, "What are the key component parts of this?"

**"Everything I have to do tomorrow"
analyzed by "business tasks"**
- *Call on customer Smith.*
- *Call on customer Jones.*
- *Call on customer Brown.*
- *Return phone calls to ABC, XYZ, MNO, and PQR customers.*
- *Develop proposals for customers White and Brown.*
- *Attempt to make appointments with these prospects: ABC, XYZ, ZZZ, AAA, and BBB.*

Now you're getting the idea. You are going to take one item, and hit it with the sledgehammer, and as a result, you're going to create a list of a bunch of items, each of which is a component of the first. That's called analyzing. And it's an essential skill for the successful 21st-century salesperson.

Prioritizing

What do you do when you have too much to do and not enough time in which to do it? If you can't do everything, you must do some things and not others. If you are going to be at all effective, you must do those things that are most important, and not do those things that are less important. In other words, you must prioritize. Like analyzing, it's an essential thinking skill for effective time management.

Here's the dictionary definition that I like the best: *Prioritizing: to rank in order of importance.* I like to further expand that with a working definition for salespeople. *Prioritizing: choosing what or who to focus on first.*

As you can imagine, you'll find yourself using this thinking skill constantly. You'll prioritize your customers and prospects during your annual planning retreat, and you'll reprioritize them several times throughout the course of the year. You'll prioritize all the sales calls that you make, as well as the possible topics and questions you ask during those sales calls. You'll prioritize in order to create effective monthly territory plans. You'll prioritize your daily and weekly tasks, your phone calls to make, appointments to set, and your office time.

When you become adept at effective time management, you won't do anything without first prioritizing it!

So, let's work with this a bit. Here's a typical situation. Your company expects you to create a certain number of new customers each year. That means that you need to see a certain number of prospects. You have a list of 125 prospects. Where do you start? Who do you call first?

This is a great time to prioritize. You know you can't call them all, let alone see them all. So you have to prioritize, to choose some to focus on first. Just like with analyzing, the starting part is a question you ask yourself. "Which of these is most important to focus on first?" As we think about this project, the first question that comes up is, "On what basis do we decide?" In other words, do we prioritize on the basis of the size of the prospects? Or what about their proximity to other accounts? Or maybe we focus first on those who are smaller and easier to see. See the problem? In order to prioritize, we need to create a basis on which to prioritize. If we prioritize this group of prospects on the basis of size, we'll have one list; while if we prioritize them on the basis of proximity to our current customers, we may have a completely different list.

The key, therefore, to effectively prioritizing, is to select the wisest, most defendable basis for the prioritization. How you do that is similar to how you went about analyzing. You create a question about your list of items, and then you simply answer that question. When you answer that question, you, in effect, prioritize the list.

For example, if you are going to prioritize your prospects on the basis of their size, you ask and answer the question, "What are the relative sizes of each of these?" If you are going to prioritize them on the basis of proximity to your current customers, you would ask and answer the question, "Which of these is within five miles of an existing customer?"

Tips from the troops...

Pause before you say "Yes." Think about how much time you are committing, and what the likely result will be.

Here's an all-purpose, universally applicable basis that you can use to prioritize almost everything in your job. It's a question that will help you make good decisions about what to focus on first. Here's the question—*What's closest to the money?*

Closest to the money means dollars of revenue received by your company. What choice, what decision, what item on the list is likely to turn into money received by your company first? And which one next? And which one after that?

Let's apply this to the prospect task. Ask the question of your 125 prospects, "Which ones of these are closest to the money?" The answer to that question provides you with your priorities—which to focus on first. Earlier, we had considered prioritizing them on the basis of size. But you know that big accounts take a lot longer to close then smaller accounts, so size is no indication of *close to the money*. And proximity to your current accounts has nothing to do with *close to the money* either. However, those accounts that will see you immediately may be closer to the money than any others, because you have an opportunity to start the sales cycle sooner.

"Which of these is likely to see me first?" As you think about that, you realize that, if you have an introduction or referral by someone else, the chances are better that the prospect will see you than if you come in cold. So, the question now becomes, "In which of these prospects can I get someone to refer me?" You look through the list, and come up with 14 prospects who are known by your current customer base. If you go to those customers and ask them to introduce you to some individual within your prospect accounts, they will likely do that.

Back to the original question, "Who to focus on first?" The answer is a further question, "Who is closest to the money?" And the answer to that is the 14 accounts in which you think you can arrange an introduction. You have just prioritized your list of prospects; you have chosen whom to focus on first by thinking about it in the right way.

Can you see what an advantage you have over your colleagues who blindly and thoughtlessly work down the list? Truly, the best salespeople are the best thinkers.

Let's apply this concept to another typical situation. You have a list of tasks to do that extends so long you can't possibly get them all done. So, you must prioritize. You understand, now, that means you must select which to focus on first, and you must do that by asking yourself the question, "Which of these is closest to the money?"

Here's a typical list of tasks for a field salesperson. Read each task, and rank it in order of closest to the money. Put a #1 in the field for the task that is closest to the money, a #2 for the next closest, and so on, until you rank all 10 tasks.

Task	Your Rank
1. Create a proposal for Smith Brothers (a good customer).	_____
2. Check on a back order for Jones.	_____
3. Make an appointment to do some training on the new product line purchased by Green Manufacturing.	_____
4. Send X product literature to prospect Brown.	_____
5. Send Y product literature to customer White.	_____
6. Get a sample of Z product and drop it off at Black.	_____
7. See the boss about a price reduction to get the business at Red.	_____
8. Call prospects Yellow, Green, and Orange to get first appointments.	_____
9. Schedule an appointment to see the PA at Blue to confirm the specs for X product.	_____
10. Get milk on the way home.	_____

Here's my choice, with an explanation of why I made that choice.

1. Highest priority: **Check on the back order.** It's closest to the money. The sooner they receive the product, the sooner you get paid, and the quicker revenue comes into the company.

2. Next highest priority: **Discount to get the business.** If you can reduce the price a bit in this account, they have promised you the business. That means that you should be able to get a Purchase Order (P.O.) in the next couple of days. That should turn into revenue soon.

3. Next highest priority: **Write up the specs.** You already have an agreement by the production engineer to use your exclusive product. After the P.A. writes up the specs, you can expect a P.O. in a week or so. That will turn into dollars before any of the remaining tasks.

4. Next highest priority: **Create a proposal.** Your good customer has already seen the product, likes it, and has moved forward in the decision-making process to the point where they are seriously considering it. The proposal is their next step. While this is pretty close to the money, it's not a sure deal yet, therefore it isn't as close as the previous tasks.

5. Next highest priority: **Arrange training.** This is a little arbitrary. You can make a good case for moving this up the priority list, as well as moving it down. I put it here, because of this line of thinking: While this won't necessarily bring immediate money, the fact is, the company is not going to reorder the new product until their people are trained. They have already purchased their beginning inventory. Once they start using the product, following your training, they can be expected to reorder. So, your work on this task will generate additional revenue in the next couple of months.

6. Next highest priority: **Get a sample of Z product and drop it off.** You've already talked with them about the product, and they have enough interest to request a sample to test. That's closer to the money then just sending literature, but further than all of the tasks above.

7. Next highest priority: **Send product literature to prospects.** They have some interest, which is why they've requested spec sheets. Customers are more likely to buy than prospects, and that's why the customer task has higher priority than the prospect.

8. Next highest priority: **Prospect calls.** Of all the sales-related tasks, this is the least likely to turn into dollars soon.

9. Lowest priority: **Get milk on the way home.** But don't forget. You need to keep the home fires warm.

Once you become comfortable with this thinking skill, you need to apply it to every aspect of your job. Don't do anything without first prioritizing it. Move out of the world of thoughtless, habitual, reactive behavior. Instead, think about it before you do it. Think right! Prioritize! Always work at what's closest to the money.

Planning

By now, you should be seeing a sequence develop. First you analyze, then you prioritize. That applies to almost every task you have. Need to decide what to do next week? Analyze first and create a master list of all the possibilities. Then prioritize them. Want to work with the customers who will get you the highest possible return on your time? First, analyze your customers and prospects, then prioritize them. Need to create a set of goals for next year? First analyze them, then prioritize.

Take any sizeable task you face, and always address it with the same skills. First you analyze, then you prioritize. First you hit with the hammer and break it into little pieces, then you decide which of those pieces to focus on first.

So, let's say that you've done those two things. Now what? Now you *plan*. *Planning,* according to the dictionary, means *to create a step-by-step series of actions.* Just like analyzing and prioritizing, planning is one of the essential thinking skills that you will use constantly, if you are going to be an effective time manager.

Salespeople, as a profession, are probably more guilty of not planning than any other professional group. There are a couple of reasons for that. First is our natural personality inclination toward action. We like to be busy, we like to have lots of things to do, people to see, places to go. And so our natural inclination is to do, before we think about doing. It's to act before we think about acting. It's to jump in the car and go, before we think about what we're going to do when we get there. It's to get on the phone and call before we think about what we are going to say when they answer.

Secondly, some of us have become very good at interpersonal communication. In other words, we're extremely confident in our ability to think on our feet to come up with the right

---

Tips from the troops...

Consider whether every call you make must be a live visit. Many calls to extablished customers can be made via telephone or e-mail, reducing the amount of drive time while still staying in touch with the customer.

---

strategies and tactics on the spur of the moment. And so we forgo, planning and in its place substitute a reliance on our spur-of-the-moment reactive capabilities. Or, as one of my former friends used to say, "Salespeople are full of B.S."

That's too bad, because planning can make the difference between a mediocre use of time, and therefore mediocre results, and an excellent use of time, and therefore, outstanding results. Good planning is one of the behaviors that separates the excellent salespeople from the mediocre. I have never met an excellent salesperson who was not a good planner.

You'll use your planning processes in almost every aspect of your job, continuously throughout the year. In the previous chapter, I discussed the planning cycle, which consisted of formal, structured planning time on this schedule:

- ▣ Annual planning retreats.

- ▣ Quarterly planning sessions of one-half to one day.

- ▣ Monthly planning session of approximately one-half day.

- ▣ Weekly plans.

- ▣ Daily preparation.

- ▣ Pre-call preparation.

In every single one of these events, you'll use your planning process. Not only that, but you'll use it as you get ready to go into the office, prior to your next formal meeting with the boss, etc. Planning is an essential thinking skill for the excellent time manager. The job of the field salesperson is so infused with planning that it may be more accurate to say that you are *always planning.*

Just like the other thinking skills, there is a basic process to planning. Once you understand it and become adept at it, you can apply that process over and over to all kinds of tasks and problems.

There are four simple steps to the planning process:

1. Assess: to define the current situation as accurately as possible.

2. Focus: to clearly define goals and objectives.

3. Process: to describe a step-by-step series of tasks that will achieve the objective.

4. Gather tools: to collect the things necessary to work the process.

Let's apply these to a typical situation. You boss held a sales meeting this morning and announced that every salesperson must get three accounts using your hot new product within the next two months. This is not optional.

It's Sunday evening and you're thinking about how you can do that. You decide to *think right*! First you analyze your customers, using the question, "Who could use your HNP (hot new product)?" You smash your customer list with that hammer, and come up with a list of 15 possibilities.

Next, you prioritize by asking the question, "Which of these are most likely to buy first?" As a result of that thinking process, you identify seven customers to focus on first.

Now you're going to plan for each of those seven accounts. You look at the highest priority account, the one that you decided to focus on first—White & Son. You apply the planning process.

Step One: Assess the situation.

On a piece of paper, one of our forms from the Time Management Tool Kit, or your computer, write out the following:

Currently using XYZ product and are having some problems. Have a good relationship with the production super and purchasing. Problem may be their long experience with XYZ—haven't used anything else in years.

What you've done is noted the critical aspects of the situation as you see it, trying to be as objective as possible. Now, you are ready to move on to the next step.

Step Two: Focus—clearly define goals and objectives.

On the next line of the form, write:

1. Get a commitment for a trial evaluation of HNP by Oct. 15.

2. Get a P.O. for their commitment to HNP by Nov. 30.

Step Three: Process—create a step-by-step action plan

What's the first thing you need to do? Then what? And after that? This is where your knowledge of the account—its people, its processes, its problems, and its culture—come together with your objectives. This is where your experience and wisdom can make all the difference.

So you think it through, and write down the following:

1. Call Joe, production supervisor, and get an appointment.

2. At that meeting:

- *Show him HNP.*

- *Give him a special offer to do an immediate evaluation (first check with the boss on what terms and deals we can offer).*

- *Get his commitment to take the product to the production committee. See if I can make a presentation to the committee. If not, equip Joe to pitch HNP to the committee.*

- *Make an appointment to follow up and execute the committee's decision.*

3. While I'm in the account, detail HNP to purchasing.

4. *Follow up on the committee meeting with Joe.*
   - *Work out the details of the trial eval. Have Joe write the requistion for purchasing.*
   - *Schedule the whole thing.*
   - *Hand walk the requisition to purchasing and get a P.O.*

That's your plan for accomplishing the first objective. As you look it over, you realize that you better put some deadlines in to make sure you can meet your boss's goals. Your plan now looks like this:

1. *Call Joe, production supervisor, tomorrow and get an appointment.* **By Sept. 15.**

2. *At that meeting:*
   - *Show him HNP.*
   - *Give him a special offer to do an immediate evaluation (first check with the boss on what terms and deals we can offer).*
   - *Get his commitment to take the product to the production committee. See if I can make a presentation to the committee. If not, equip Joe to pitch HNP to the committee.*
   - *Make an appointment to follow up and execute the committee's decision.*

3. *While I'm in the account, detail HNP to purchasing.*
   By Sept. 15.

4. *Follow up on the committee meeting with Joe.*
   - *Work out the details of the trial eval. Have Joe write the requisition for purchasing.*
   - *Schedule the whole thing.*
   - *Hand walk the requisition to purchasing and get a P.O.* **By Oct. 15.**

At this point, you have done some powerful and effective work. However, you are not done yet. Time to address the last of the four steps to the planning process.

Step Four: Gather the necessary tools.

A tool is anything you use to help you accomplish your plan. So, you look at each step of the process and ask yourself the question, "What do I need to do this?"

1. At that meeting: **By Sept. 15.**

- *Show him HNP.*

- *Give him a special offer to do an immediate evaluation (first check with the boss on what terms and deals we can offer).*

- *Get his commitment to take the product to the production committee. See if I can make a presentation to the committee. If not, equip Joe to pitch HNP to the committee.*

- *Make an appointment to follow up and execute the committee's decision.*

Tools: 1. HNP literature—enough for every committee member.

2. HNP sample.

3. Details of special deals.

2.. While I'm in the account, detail HNP to purchasing.
                By Sept. 15.

Tools: 1. HNP literature.

2. Pricing and availability info.

3. Cross reference competitive numbers to make the conversion easier.

I know what you're thinking. "Isn't this a lot of work? Doesn't it take a lot of time?" *Yes. Of course.* But if you take this time and do this work, then everything else goes so much smoother, and you are far more effective than if you hadn't done it. Remember the rule: *Spend 20 percent of your time planning for the other 80 percent.* You can choose to not do this. You can be like most of the mediocre salespeople in the world. You can allow yourself to become reactive and sucked into a routine of frenzied low-effectiveness activity. Or you can choose to work far more effectively by implementing the disciplines of thinking about it before you do it, and thinking about it in the right way. It's a free country. It's your choice.

Imaging

Here's another powerful thinking process that is an amazing tool in the hands of a skilled practitioner. *Imaging* is the process of seeing, in your mind's eye, the specific situation for which you are preparing, and to practice that situation mentally. It differs from *imagining*, which is more like daydreaming—it's more free flowing and allows for all kinds of possibilities. Imaging is very focused. You mentally see the situation for which you are preparing, and you mentally rehearse your part of it.

It is based on the observation that your mind doesn't recognize the difference between a real and an imagined event. That's why you wake up sweating from a nightmare. While the nightmare was imaginary, your body and mind reacted as if it were real.

If that is true for negative and scary things like nightmares, it is also true for more positive things, like practicing sales calls or portions of them. Because your mind works much faster than your body does, you can practice a 30-minute presentation in just a few moments. Practicing it mentally is almost as good as practicing it physically.

I'm a professional speaker. When I am preparing a new presentation, for example, I'll always rehearse it a number of times mentally. It's a good use of hotel room time. Better than watching CNN headlines for the sixth time. I just close my eyes, and see myself giving the presentation, word for word.

When I come to a part I'm unsure of, I'll stop, review my notes and then continue on. I can review a 60-minute keynote speech two or three times in the course of half an hour.

So it is for you. You can mentally rehearse a sales call, or a portion of it, in a few minutes. If it's a big call, rehearse it the night before. Find a quiet and secluded place, close your eyes, and then put yourself mentally in the situation. See yourself shaking hands, starting the conversation, using your literature or AV aids. Watch yourself say every word.

Don't worry if you drift off from time to time. When you find yourself thinking about something else, just stop and move back to the presentations. Don't worry too much about the mental scenery surrounding your sales call. The important thing to focus on is your behavior. Watch yourself ask questions, respond to comments and questions, and present your program or offer. See yourself respond to objections and questions.

If you are making a small, routine sales call take a few moments in the car before the call and image yourself making the call. If you have an important or new phone call to make, do the same. Close your eyes; see yourself making the phone call. Image every response you are likely to experience, and then see yourself replying.

It really takes very little time, and will add immeasurably to your effectiveness. It's one of the best uses of your time, as you continue to work within the arena of careful preparation.

The more prepared you are, the more effective you will be. That makes preparation an excellent use of your time, and thorough preparation is one of the secrets of effective sales time management.

This kind of exercise and the discipline that results from it provides you two powerful benefits. First, you will be more effective because you will have practiced the thing you are preparing to do, whether it be the question, the presentation, or the whole sales call. The mental practice means that you will be better at it.

Second, and just as important, you will be more confident. If you are confident, you think better, and you put the customer more at ease. Additionally, the customer reads your confidence as less risk for him or her. The more confident you are, the easier it is for your customer to say yes to you.

Confidence is good. Confidence comes from only two things: experience or preparation. If you haven't made this sales call 100 times before, you probably don't have sufficient experience. Substitute preparation. Use *imaging.*

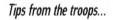

Tips from the troops...

Use a small notebook that will fit into a shirt pocket. Divide it into four equal sections—two at the top and two at the bottom. Title the uppermost left column "Calls." The column to the right title "New Customers." Title one of the remaining spaces "To Do's" and the final space, "Notes." Organize your day, every day on this one piece of paper.

Reflecting

If only things always went the way you had planned! Life would be so much more fun. You'd earn more money, be more successful, and realize more enjoyment in your job. Your mother-in-law would like you. Your spouse would think you are perfect. But as you know, no matter how well you plan, things don't always go the way you had planned.

When that happens, it's helpful to analyze what went wrong and what to do differently next time. That's one of my favorite thinking processes: *Reflecting.*

Here's my definition: Reflecting is the process of thinking seriously—contemplating and pondering—usually about something you have done.

It is one of the most useful of the time management thinking processes, because it saves you time by preventing you from repeating a mistake. So much of our time is wasted doing the wrong things in the wrong ways. If we can eliminate any of this, then we're making better use of our time. Reflecting is the process that does that for us.

You reflect when you think about something that you have done (the past), make some conclusions about what you did well and did not do well, and then determine to do some things differently in the future.

Here's an example. You just completed a sales call and are sitting in your car, making some notes. Ask yourself this question, "Did I accomplish what I wanted to?" You answer yourself, "Partially. I got an understanding of their production problems with the competitive machine—that was one of my objectives. But I couldn't get them to commit to an evaluation of my new model."

Next question, "Why or why not?" You think to yourself, "Let's see. Bill, the production supervisor, seemed really eager to talk about his problems with the competitive machine. A couple of open-ended questions on my part, and a really interested attitude were all it took to get him talking. That was good. Now, why didn't they commit to an evaluation of my new model? What happened?"

You think more deeply. "After Bill finished explaining his production problems, I said that our new model would solve all those problems. I gave him a piece of literature, and I asked him if we could bring it in and let him evaluate it. At that point, he got sort of uncomfortable, started making excuses, and was done with the conversation. Why was that?"

You reflect some more. "I suppose that he just wasn't ready to evaluate it. Bringing a new machine into his production area would probably upset his routine, and cost him some extra time. Maybe he was thinking he had enough problems without introducing something new. Hey, maybe he didn't believe me that it would solve his problems." Having thought to this point, you now ask this question, "So, what could you have done differently to cause a different outcome?"

Your answer, as you think to yourself, is: "Maybe I shouldn't jump immediately from his problems to asking for an evaluation. Maybe I should have asked Bill what he saw as the next step. Maybe I should have let him have some time to think through what he wanted to do about the new model."

Now you get to the key question: "What should I do differently the next time I'm in a similar situation? I should pause after I present the new model, and let the customer ask questions and think it through. When I immediately ask for an evaluation, I put him on the spot and force him to take a position. I should ask him how he would like to proceed instead of just assuming that he wants to evaluate the machine. After all, he's the one who has to make all the arrangements. He knows what he has to work with. That way, we can keep the project moving forward."

Here's what you did:

1. You chose an event, in this case a sales call.

2. You evaluated how successful it was by asking yourself the question, "Did I accomplish what I wanted to?"

3. You identified some things that you could have done differently when you answered the questions, "What happened?" and "Why?"

4. You then identified a correction in your behavior when you asked yourself the question, "What should I do differently the next time?"

Pretty simple. It only takes a few minutes. As a result of this focused thinking process, you will be more effective next time. And each time you add quality to your interactions with your customers, you more effectively use your time and theirs.

Reflecting is one of the most valuable thinking processes because it causes you to constantly improve. It's a common discipline of the most effective time managers and the best salespeople.

You can, and should, apply this process in a number of specific ways. Remember the thinking cycle we established in our discussion of Management Secret Two—*think about it before you do it.* Each of those occasions is a time to apply the discipline of reflecting.

Let's review that cycle, and see where we should be using this thinking process:

- Annual planning retreat of one to three days.

- Quarterly planning sessions of one-half to one day.

- Monthly planning session of approximately one-half day.

- Weekly plans.

- Daily preparation.

- Pre-call preparation.

- Post-call reflection.

In your annual planning retreat, you ought to reflect on the past year and your results. Start with the question, "Last year, did I accomplish what I wanted to?" Then, follow the same questioning sequence. Ask yourself:

- "Why or why not?"

- "What exactly happened?"

- "What could I have done differently to achieve different results?"

- "What should I do differently next year?"

Repeat this process in your quarterly, monthly, and weekly planning sessions. Just substitute the appropriate time frame in your beginning question. So, instead of "Last year, did I accomplish what I wanted to?" your question should begin with, "Last month"..."last week," etc.

You'll find that thinking through this question sequence—reflecting—on a disciplined and regular basis will become one of the best things you do, as it always leads to some positive change in your behavior. And that change in your behavior will allow you to be more effective in your use of time.

To implement this management secret:

1. Pick one "A" account to focus on, and work through each of the steps of the "think right" process: *Analyze, prioritize, plan*. Capture your work in writing.

2. Repeat this process a few times, until you begin to automatically think in this way.

3. Write down the questions that prompt the *reflecting* process. Or use the forms in our Time Management Tool Kit. Pick one or two sales calls, and spend a few moments in the car after the call asking yourself these questions. Capture your answers in writing.

4. Now that you have worked through these two exercises and become comfortable with the processes, make it a point to continue to repeat the process so that it becomes a habit.

5. Follow the same process for *imaging*. Decide to do it. Focus on one day and remind yourself to image each sales call that day. After the day, reflect on the success you had. Then decide to do it every day and instill it as a habit into your routine.

The Fourth Time Management Secret:

Prioritize Your Customers and Prospects!

There is probably no one area of your business that is more important for you to prioritize than your customers and prospects. Fortunately, it's also the area of your job that will make the biggest impact on your performance. From my personal experience as a salesperson for more than 30 years, plus my experience in consulting with more than 300 companies and training tens of thousands of salespeople, I'm convinced that this one area holds more potential for making dramatic and immediate changes in your results than any other.

It's the first consideration for working effectively. Becoming more effective starts with painting the right house, and that means deciding in which customers and prospects to invest your precious time.

Start with an attitude check. Too often, salespeople spend time with customers who like them, or who are easy to see, or who have become friends. These are nice, and certainly there is a place in every sales territory for those kinds of customers. But if those customers aren't high potential, then investing time in them isn't smart.

Other salespeople allow their days to be controlled by the problems, interests, and whims of their customers without regard to their potential. They spend all day responding and reacting to whomever is on the phone or asking for their time. Again, there is a place for this, but those salespeople who allow this reaction to customer inquiries to shape their days are not working smart.

Tips from the troops...

When you leave a voice mail message, make sure you state exactly when someone can call you back in order to reach you. Avoid telephone tag.

83

Working smart requires an attitude. The attitude is this: I will make *cold-blooded business decisions* about where to invest my time. Why cold-blooded? Because we're naturally drawn to people who are easy and comfortable for us to visit. We like to be among people where we are warmly regarded. But just because a group of customers makes us comfortable doesn't mean that we should spend our time there. We need to eliminate that natural propensity for the comfortable call by instilling an attitude of cold-bloodedness. We need to make decisions about where to invest our time on more logical, hard and fast money-related criteria. We've got to apply cold-blooded logic to protect ourselves from ourselves, and to make the most effective use of our most precious asset: our selling time.

Let's consider this together. Some prospects and customers have more potential than others. But what is the implication for our behavior? If some prospects and customers have more potential than others, shouldn't we then spend the most time with the highest potential?

Of course. That makes sense. Did you spend most of your time last week with your highest potential customers and prospects? Probably not.

There is a basic principle to human labor that says most of your results will come from only a small portion of your market. You are familiar with the Paretto Principle, for example, which states that 80 percent of your sales will come from 20 percent of your customers. A number of years ago, I came across a similar principle put forth in the book *Everything I Need to Know About Success, I Learned in the Bible* by Richard Gaylord Briley. Briley described the 5/50 principle, which states that 50 percent of the jobs and affluence in a society will be generated by the work of 5 percent of the population. I've applied that to businesses and sales territories and found it to be invariably true—50 percent of the business comes from 5 percent of the customers.

My personal experience supports this insight. In my consulting practice, on about a dozen occasions, I've been a part of a project in which the client analyzed the net contribution to company profits by each customer. This is an attempt to allocate all the company's costs to all its customers in a fair and objective way, and to determine which customers are most profitable for the company on a net (not gross) profit basis. In every case, the results have been the same: About 10 percent of the customers provide all the profit for the company, and subsidize the business for the other 90 percent!

This project is a little different than what we're talking about. It focuses on analyzing the net profitability for the entire company, while we are discussing your personal return on investment for just your sales territory. Regardless, the principle is the same. The overwhelming majority of your business will potentially come from a handful of your customers. So, when we say some prospects and customers have more potential than others, what we really mean is that 5 to 20 percent of your customers have 50 to 80 percent of your potential.

When we say that you should spend the most time with the highest potential, we mean, you should spend the most time with those high-potential 5 to 20 percent of your account base.

This doesn't mean that you forget most of your customers and ignore the majority of your prospects. What it does mean, however, is that you become guided by this very practical rule for cold-blooded decisions:

> **Spend 50 percent of your selling time on the high-potential accounts, and 50 percent of your time on everyone else.**

Why you get better results by focusing on a few high-potential accounts

Suppose you have $1 million in potential in one high-potential account and the same potential equally spread in 10 lower-potential accounts. How many hours will it take to make one call on each of those 10 accounts? Include drive time, time spent making appointments, waiting time, preparation time, and so on. How long will it take you to call on that one high-potential account? Considerably less. Even if you were to call on 10 people in that one high potential account, your total investment in time will still be less. Just from an efficiency perspective, it makes good sense to focus on high-potential accounts.

Once you have established a presence in a high-potential account, it's easier to sell. You can leverage your relationships more easily in larger, high-potential accounts. Get one person on your side, advocating for you, and he or she can spread the good word about you quickly to half a dozen people. It is like the pebble dropped into the lake causing ripples to move outward from the center. Your good contact is like the pebble, spreading increasing ripples of good press about you. Get one good small-account person on your side, and they don't tell anyone, because there is no one to tell. A pebble dropped into a glass of water won't make ripples for long because there isn't enough water around it. You can't leverage your relationship like you can in larger accounts.

Defining high-potential

In order to implement this strategy, you need to have a workable definition of "high potential." Many salespeople labor under a big misconception when it comes to potential. They define potential in terms of history. In other words, if I asked you to show me your high potential accounts, you'd pull out a computer report showing sales history. In reality, however, history has little to do with potential. Just because an account has been a good customer in the past does not necessarily mean that it is a high-potential customer for the future. Potential describes what they could buy in the *future,* while sales reports record the *past.*

The second common misconception is thinking that potential is only measured in dollars of sales. In other words, an account that could buy $500,000 from you is automatically thought of as having more potential than an account that could buy $250,000. It isn't necessarily so.

Real potential is not measured by one number, it's measured by a ratio of two. High potential is the ratio of the likelihood of dollars received compared to the amount of time invested in order to achieve those dollars.

High potential = **The ratio of the likelihood of dollars received compared to the amount of time invested in order to achieve those dollars.**

$$\text{Potential} = \frac{\text{Likelihood of dollars received}}{\text{Time invested}}$$

Let's consider two accounts. Smith Brothers theoretically could buy $500,000 from you next year, while Ajax Manufacturing could buy half as much—$250,000. If we only look at total dollars, Smith has more potential. But that view is too simplistic and doesn't reflect the reality of the situation. Suppose the real situation is this: Smith Brothers has a long-standing contract with one of your competitors. That sole-source contract is not due to expire for three more years. Not only that, but your competitor and Smith Brothers are extremely close in other ways, as the CEOs of Smith Brothers and your competitor are brothers-in-law. You can spend hundreds of hours calling on Smith Brothers. Chances are, you are not going to see a penny in additional sales.

Ajax, on the other hand, has no such affinity for your competitors. In fact, the personal relationships between you and the key players there are very good. Their business philosophy is very close to yours, and you have a good history of relationships between your company and theirs. You know several people in key roles inside the organization, and you've even had lunch with the CEO.

Now, considering the reality of the situation between the two accounts, where is the most promising investment in your time? Is it Smith, with its larger dollar potential? Or is it Ajax, with its smaller potential volume? It would take me about two seconds to select Ajax. Why? Because potential is not one number, it's the ratio of two. Because potential is defined by the likelihood of dollars returned for your investment of time. Because 10 hours, selling time invested in Ajax will bring you far more dollars returned than the same investment in Smith. It's not how much they can buy, it's how much they are *likely* to buy in return for your investment of selling time in them.

Tips from the troops...

Call yourself and leave a voice mail message. Then listen critically. Would you return a call to this person? You can improve your results by practicing and refining your messages as you lisen to your messages to yourself.

This is a keystone concept in your battle to become more effective. Many of the decisions you make will rest on this understanding. Once you are comfortable with this idea—potential isn't dollars, potential is the likelihood of dollars returned for time invested—the question then becomes, "How do I determine that potential?"

Determining potential

Potential, as we defined it earlier, is comprised of two elements: *quantified purchasing capability (QPC), and partnerability.*

Quantified purchasing capability (QPC) is the objective measurement of how much of your product the account could buy if they bought everything they could from you. It's usually calculated in annual terms. Obviously each account has different capability to purchase your product or service. Let's work with this to completely understand it.

One component of this has to do with how much they could buy from you. It has to do with their capability to purchase the products or services that you sell. For example, you may be selling radio advertising. Jones Manufacturers has an advertising budget of $20,000 for the next year, and XYZ Consulting group has a budget of $40,000. However, you don't sell all types of advertising, you sell only radio advertising. And Jones has decided to put 100 percent of their budget, or $20,000 into radio advertising, while XYZ has decided on 5 percent of their budget, or $2,000, for radio. Jones Manufacturing, while smaller and having a smaller advertising budget, actually has a QPC that is 10 times larger than the bigger and more prestigious XYZ Consulting group. In terms of QPC, Jones far outranks XYZ. The first rule for calculating QPC, then, is understanding that it only measures the account's ability to purchase **your** products and services.

What about the account that is already buying everything they can from you? Does it have any QPC? Sure. Remember, QPC is an annual measure of how much they can buy from you in the future. So, for example, you may be selling cleaning supplies to Quik-Clean Janitorial Services. Over the years, you've built a great relationship with them, and they buy everything from you. Last year, they bought $75,000 worth of your stuff. They expect to grow their business this year, and they will probably buy $80,000 of your supplies. What's the QPC? $80,000. QPC is a measurement of how much of your products or services the account could buy annually, if they bought everything they could from you. It focuses on the future, not the past. So, when you calculate QPC, you don't dwell on what they bought in the past, you calculate their capability to purchase in the future.

Notice the word "quantified" in the title of this measurement. The word is there for a purpose. It means that you have some logical, defendable way of determining how much they could buy from you. Too many salespeople rely on intuition and gut reactions, and are often misguided. In the 21st-century economy, you must be better than that. "It looks pretty big" is not a logical, defendable measure of purchasing capability.

How do you measure QPC? The easiest way is to ask the account and have them give you an honest and accurate answer. In some industries, and with some accounts, this is the norm. You may be selling production machinery, for example. When you ask the purchasing agent what their budget is for capital expenditures on production equipment next year, they may just tell you. Or you may sell, as I did, hospital supplies. When you ask the materials manager how much they spent for surgical gloves last year, he could probably tell you, down to the penny. Then, you could ask him if he expects that to increase, decrease, or remain flat, and by what percentage. Do the math, and you'd have a very good measurement of QPC for surgical gloves.

While asking is always the easiest way to get this number, it doesn't always work. Some accounts don't know, and others know but they won't tell you. In those cases, you have to use other means.

One way is to mathematically calculate the QPC based on some formula driven by a measurement that you do know. In my days of selling hospital supplies, for example, we knew that, on the average, an occupied acute care bed in a hospital used a certain amount (say $20) of needles and syringes per day. If you were calling on a 300-bed hospital, and you knew they averaged a 90-percent occupancy, then you could calculate how much they would spend on needles and syringes each year. Let's do it. Three hundred beds times 90 percent equals 270 beds occupied on the average day. Multiply that by 365 days a year, and that equals 98,550 occupied bed days. Multiply that by the $20 per day, and the QPC for needles and syringes in that hospital is $1,971,000.

Where did we get those numbers? Trade journals and industry surveys yielded the $20 per day number. The annual report or hospital Website may tell you how many beds the hospital has, as well as its average occupancy rate. So, in this case, a few minutes of research unearthed a calculated QPC number. We calculated the QPC mathematically, based on some numbers we did know. We could do that for every category of product we sold without ever having said hello to the first person in the hospital itself.

One of my clients, whose company sells industrial supplies, calculates the QPC based on the number of cars in the employee parking lot, and the type of business. For example, he knows that in a tool and die shop, each car in the employee parking lot means a certain number, let's say $1,000, of annual cutting tools usage. So, a tool and die shop with 15 cars in the employee parking lot will typically buy $15,000 worth of cutting tools.

As a variation on this, you can infer the QPC deductively, based on some numbers that you know about a larger group. My company sells sales training. Let's say we're trying to calculate the QPC for sales training for a medium-sized distributor of fasteners. We know from industry surveys, for example, that most companies spend between 1.5 percent and 3.5 percent of their payroll on training. We also know that the average fastener distributor salesperson makes about $50,000 per year. We know from D&B reports that this particular company has sales of about $30 million. Finally we know, again from industry surveys, that the average salesperson in this industry manages a territory of about $1.75 million. Okay, let's do the math. $30 million divided by $1.75 million yields a likely number of 17 salespeople. Multiplying the 17 by $50,000 yields a likely sales payroll of $850,000. Let's use a 2 percent estimate of how much they are likely to spend on training. That's the midpoint in the 1.5 to 3.5 percent spectrum. So, $850,000 times 2-percent yields a QPC of $17,000. What's the QPC for sales training in this account? $17,000.

Now, granted that number isn't as accurate as having the account tell us what their budget is (if they have one). However, it's significantly better than shooting from the hip and saying, "They're a pretty good size." It meets our criteria: it's logical, defendable, and quantifiable.

One level deeper

We can be even more precise than that, taking our understanding of the customer's QPC to another deeper level. Let's try to calculate the customer's QPC per *category* of product or service that we sell.

There's a powerful reason for this. The more precisely you can measure the prospect, or customer's QPC, the more sharply you can define your strategy, and the more effective you will be. Remember, one of the rallying cries of good sales time management is *focus, focus, focus*. You can't focus well if you don't know what the target is. Once you have a precise view of the target, you can more easily focus on it.

Let's assume that you sell computer equipment. Your product offerings include these categories: PCs, printers and peripherals, and maintenance services. You've called on Able Consulting Group and discovered that they just invested in new PCs throughout the office. QPC in the PC category is $0. However, they held off on adding new printers, and are planning to upgrade 20 printers in the next six months. You calculate 20 times an average of $250 each, and that equals a QPC for printers and peripherals of $5,000. You also know that the company has 50 PCs and that the average annual Preventative Maintenance fee per PC is $50. So, 50 PCs times $50 equals a QPC of $2,500 for services.

Your analysis of this account's QPC looks like this:

Category	Annual QPC
PCs	$0
Printers and peripherals	$5,000
Service	$2,500
Total	$7,500

Tips from the troops...

Make sure you clarify what your customer or colleague is saying. Paraphrase and repeat it back to them before you decide to act on it. You'll be amazed how many times you didn't get it exactly right, causing you wasted efforts and wasted time.

Understanding how much QPC there is, and in which categories helps you to do two things: Make cold-blooded business decisions about how much time you should invest here, and develop a strategy for getting that business. Knowing that the business is in printers and service will generate one strategy, while if the business were in PCs, you'd formulate a different strategy.

Calculating partnerability

Understanding QPC is essential. But that's only half of the issue. Remember our previous discussion of Smith Brothers and Ajax Manufacturing? Smith had twice the QPC of Ajax, but there was virtually no chance of getting that business. That was because of factors other than QPC. In the case of Smith Brothers, the account had a long-term, sole-source contract with your competitor, and the CEOs of Smith and your competitor were brothers-in-law. So, it wasn't the QPC that influenced our decision about that account, it was a combination of other, softer issues that lead us to the conclusion that we should not invest major selling time in Smith Brothers.

We can lump all of those other, softer, more subjective factors into a measurement I call *partnerability*. The practical potential of an account is part QPC and part *partnerability*. *Partnerability* is based on subjective analysis about the likelihood of the account eventually becoming a partner. The issues that comprise partnerability are things like:

- ▣ How is the chemistry between the two companies, and between yourself and your contact people?

- ▣ Is the account just a price buyer, or is it open to creative proposals from you?

- ▣ Is it a progressive, growing organization?

Notice that these are subjective, softer issues than the hard numbers of QPC. However, they are just as important to you in determining the account's practical potential.

You may have one account that has huge quantifiable potential, like Smith Brothers, but because of the philosophy or personalities of the decision-makers, no foreseeable *partnerability*. That account would not be a high-potential account.

Let's say you have a very large account that offers tremendous potential. At the same time, you know the business is very competitive, that every other competitor is working for that account. The account has long used one of your competitors and he appears to be very solid in the account. The account ranks low in potential partnerability. A sober assessment means that you'll have to invest countless hours, maybe years, before you can have any realistic opportunity to sell anything.

On the other hand, what if you have a much smaller account that you have a realistic possibility of closing some business with after just a couple of calls? Which one would rank higher on the "potential dollars returned for time invested" scale? Obviously, the second does.

That's the kind of cold-blooded analysis that helps you organize your time in a very effective way.

One key is to have some way to calculate partnerability that is more defendable and quantifiable than just a salesperson's intuitive hunch.

Measuring partnerability

It has been my experience that a salesperson can visit an account once or twice, and make some valuable observations about the partnerability of that account—the likelihood of that account developing into a partner one day. In my seminars, I'll often ask the group to develop a list of plusses and minuses. Plusses are characteristics or behaviors of the account that *increase* the likelihood of the account developing into a partner. Minuses are the characteristics or behaviors of the account that *decrease* the likelihood that it will one day develop into a partner.

I. Good product/service fit

Let's say you offer 10 products. Brill Brothers Manufacturing company can use all 10, and all of them are important to their business. Jones Industries can use two of your 10, and neither of the two is really central to their business. Who is the better product/service fit? Clearly, it's Brill Brothers. Notice the two issues for product/service fit:

1. The degree to which an account can use your product or service offerings.

2. The degree to which those products/services are important to them.

2. Personal chemistry

This speaks to the personal relationship between you and the customer. On one hand, a professional salesperson ought to be able to build positive business relationships with anyone. On the other, it's a whole lot easier with some people. If most of the important people at Brill Brothers like you, are comfortable with you, and trust you, it's going to be much more likely that they will grow into a partner with you than Jones Industries, where there is just a little tension between you and most of the important people there. The personal chemistry isn't the same.

3. Good management

You don't invest your money in stocks that are doomed, and you don't invest your time in losers, either. If a company appears to be well organized and well managed, chances are it's going to grow or at least survive. On the other hand, those that are characterized by high employee turnover, bad attitudes, sloppy and unorganized facilities, and no plans are likely to struggle in the future.

4. Compatible philosophy

Some accounts are strictly price buyers. That's great if your organization strives to be the low-cost provider in commodity markets. You'd have a compatible philosophy. However, if your company positions itself as a value-added provider, or the high-quality choice, than you are never going to be comfortable with, or important to, the "buy the lowest price no matter what" philosophy. The more compatible your philosophies are, the greater the likelihood that will develop into a partner one day.

5. Personal respect and accessibility

In some accounts, all vendor salespeople are viewed as "peddlers" and dealt with accordingly. These are the accounts that give you 15 minutes in the conference room with a junior purchasing agent and then dismiss you. Others give you the plant tour, show you their future plans, introduce you to the VPs, and solicit your thoughts and ideas. They see you whenever you say you have something of value for them, and they respect your insights.

6. Pay well

It's a real waste of time to invest high-quality selling efforts in an account, successfully solve some of their problems and achieve a good sale, only to discover that your credit department won't approve it. Or worse yet, they do approve it, but the account doesn't pay. Better to try to discern that before you invest a lot of your time in them.

7. Industry or company-specific items

There can be a number of very specific issues that are important to your industry or your company. For example, one of my clients was a division of a Fortune 500 company. One of their criteria was whether or not the account owned equipment produced by one of the other divisions of the company. If so, it would be easier to talk with them and specify their supplies. If not, it would be more difficult.

Another client was a regional petroleum supplier. One of their criteria was the distance from the customer to their nearest distribution facility. Because of the relative importance of freight costs, if the account were geographically close to their facility and far away from a competitor's, that was good. The opposite was bad.

To implement this strategy, take the six general characteristics discussed earlier, and mesh them with at least four criteria that you create. These new criteria should be specific to your company or industry.

If you did that, you'd have a list of 10 criteria. You could rate every one of your customers on each of those 10 criteria. Think of a scale from zero to 10, with zero indicating that worst expression of that criteria, and 10 the greatest. For example, let's apply the criteria of "good management" to Cool Inc., one of your accounts. This account is progressive, always looking for the next advantage, and willing to listen to any good ideas. On the other hand, it's a family-held business, and the CEO is

Tips from the troops...

Have lunch with prospects. This is one of your best uses of time. You'll eliminate the need for an additional sales call during the day, and you'll develop a more personal relationship.

dictatorial. He does have some professional managers reporting to him, however, and that helps. Turnover is a bit of a problem because of the CEO's abrasiveness. All in all, you decide that the positives outweigh the negatives on this issue, and you give Cool, Inc. a rating of seven on the good management criteria scale.

Do this for every criteria, account by account, and you'll come up with a way to measure and compare the "partnerability" of each account.

Here's an example of a set of criteria developed and applied to Cool Inc. We're assuming that you are selling advertising, so our industry-specific criteria will reflect that focus.

Rating for: Cool, Inc. by: Mary Salesrep Jan 4, 2002

1. Good fit	9
2. Personal chemistry	7
3. Management	10
4. Compatible philosophy	9
5. Personal respect and accessibility	9
6. Pay well	9
7. Aggressive growth plans	9
8. Positive history with us	7
9. Ability to use products from our other divisions	3
10. Open to our input	5
Total	77

Putting the two together

Now, let's combine these two measurements in a simple, easy method and use them to calculate the potential of each of your accounts. At this point, you have done two things: You've developed a measurement of the account's QPC, and you have rated them on "partnerability."

On a yellow pad if you're a paper person, or a spreadsheet if you are electronic, list the names of your accounts in a column. Include those suspects and prospects that you are acquainted with.

In the next column, give them a rating for their partnerability. Use a zero to 100 scale. So, if you created 10 "partnerability" measurements and you rated each account on every one of the 10, on a one to 10 scale, you'd have a number that was the sum of those scores.

We'll use the example below, using just five accounts. In your work, you should list all of your accounts.

Account	Partnerability
Able Consulting	45
Ajax	91
Smith Brothers	72
Jones	12
Brill Brothers	61
Cool, Inc.	97

Now, we're going to enter, in the next column, the QPC for each account. We've completed it in our example below.

Account	Partnerability	QPC
Able Consulting	45	$1,450,000
Ajax	91	$647,000
Smith Brothers	72	$129,000
Jones	12	$2,100,000
Brill Brothers	61	$759,000
Cool, Inc.	97	$1,200,000

Rating QPC

Turn the dollar values into zero to 100 ratings. Let's take the QPC and lay it out in a column, with the largest number at the top and then ordered below with the next largest:

$2,100,000

$1,450,000

$1,200,000

$759,000

$647,000

$129,000

Now, we're going to assign a zero to 100 rating to each of the dollar amounts. Give the largest QPC a 100, and the smallest a 10. So, our columns now look like this:

$2,100,000	100
$1,450,000	
$1,200,000	
$759,000	
$647,000	
$129,000	10

Now you know the range from top to bottom. Trying to be as accurate as possible, assign each of the remaining dollar amounts a rating from 10 to 100 that reflects their relative size. Don't worry about being absolutely accurate. It's probably not worth developing mathematical models for. Just estimate, based on the difference between that number and the top number. Here's how I would do the remaining number in this example.

$2,100,000	100
$1,450,000	90
$1,200,000	85
$759,000	50
$647,000	47
$129,000	10

Now, carry those zero to 100 ratings over to the main spreadsheet and enter them next to the dollar amounts, so our spreadsheet now looks like this.

Account	Partnerability	QPC	0-100
Able Consulting	45	$1,450,000	90
Ajax	91	$647,000	47
Smith Brothers	72	$129,000	10
Jones	12	$2,100,000	100
Brill Brothers	61	$759,000	50
Cool, Inc.	97	$1,200,000	85

Finally, add the partnerabililty rating to the QPC rating and list the sum in the column marked "Total." For example, we're going to take Able Consulting's 45 rating of partnerability and add it to its 90 rating of QPC to arrive at a total of 135.

Account	Partnerability	QPC	0-100	Total
Able Consulting	45	$1,450,000	90	135
Ajax	91	$647,000	47	138
Smith Brothers	72	$129,000	10	82
Jones	12	$2,100,000	100	112
Brill Brothers	61	$759,000	50	111
Cool, Inc.	97	$1,200,000	85	182

Let's consider the numbers that we've developed. Clearly, Cool is the highest potential account, even though it doesn't have the largest QPC. It stands apart from the rest, in a class of its own, with a rating almost twice as large as the next largest. Interestingly, it turns out that the customer with the largest QPC, Jones, is really a low-priority account.

Developing ABC categories

What do we do with this information? Use it to categorize these accounts into three categories: A, B, and C. When we're finished, the number of A accounts will be approximately 5 to 20 percent of the total number of accounts rated. So, for example, if you have a total of 50 accounts, somewhere between two and five of them will be A accounts. If you have 100 total accounts, approximately five to 20 will fall into the A category.

So, your first step is to identify the top 5 to 20 percent, the A accounts. In our example, above, we have one A account, Cool, Inc.

Once we've identified the A accounts, we can then go down to the Cs and gather them into a category. This is typically the lowest 20 to 50 percent of the total. Again, if you have 50 accounts, somewhere between 10 and 25 will be Cs. If you have 100 accounts, approximately 20 to 50 will be Cs. So, step two is identifying the lowest group. In our example, we've identified Smith, Jones, and Brill as Cs.

All those that are left, usually about 20 to 40 percent of the total, will be Bs. In our example, that leaves us with Able and Ajax. Our work has led us to this categorization:

A accounts	B Accounts	C Accounts
Cool, Inc.	Able	Smith
	Ajax	Jones
		Brill

Growth and maintenance accounts

After you have done your initial analysis, and you reflect on the results, you may notice that, in some of your accounts, you may already enjoy almost all of the business. Let's say that you look at an account, for example, that has $100,000 of QPC, and compare it to last year's sales in that account, which were $95,000. It's clear that you are not going to gain much more sales volume in that account. An account like this, in which you enjoy most of the business, is *a maintenance* account. In other words, your job is to maintain the business you already have, not necessarily to grow it. This has significant impact on your time management decisions, because maintenance accounts usually take less time than growth accounts. The question you ask yourself as you begin to strategize and plan your time is, "What do I need to do to maintain the business in this account?"

Growth accounts, on the other hand, are those customers in which you still have significant unrealized QPC. If, for example, an account has a QPC of $100,000, but you currently enjoy only $15,000 of that potential, then you have a lot of opportunity to grow the business. If you compare your future investment of time in these two accounts, you will probably spend more time in the growth account and less time in the maintenance account, even though they both have the same QPC.

That brings us to the second guideline for effectively prioritizing your customers and prospects: Spend less time in the maintenance accounts so that you can invest more time in the growth accounts.

Put this together with the previous rule: Spend 50 percent of your time in the high-potential accounts.

Now you have a system of making decisions about the effective use of your time. This system will transform your results.

Tips from the troops...

Visualize every sales call before you make it. Think about what you want to achieve, and consider possible questions and answers. Your sales calls will become far more effective for you, as well as your customer.

To implement this management secret:

1. Methodically collect defendable and accurate QPC numbers for all your prospects and customers.

2. If appropriate, break the total QPC number per account into categories.

3. Use those numbers to create a zero to 100 rating for every account.

4. Develop a list of 10 partnerability criteria. You may want to modify it by market segment.

5. Use the criteria to create a zero to 100 partnerability rating for every account.

6. Combine the two ratings into one total number. (Or use the spreadsheet we have created in our Time Management Tool Kit.)

7. Use that number to classify each account into one of three categories: A, B, or C.

8. Spend 50 percent of your time on the A accounts, and 50 percent on the others.

The Fifth Time Management Secret:

Stay on Top of the Flow!

It would be easier if a salesperson's days were stable and predictable. Then many of the guidelines articulated by the generic time management books would apply.

Unfortunately, that's not the case. While it is important to thoroughly plan the day, it is just as important to recognize that some days don't go according to plan. There are many days that are like a fast-moving, swirling stream. Customers call with urgent problems. People aren't there for their appointments. New issues come up and take more time. Customers' agenda are longer then expected. The boss calls with an urgent request. You know the drill. Many days, in spite of our best plans, things just don't go the way we expect.

If you're caught in rapids like these, you can allow them to buffet you around and take you wherever they push you, or you can constantly check your location and make fine-tuning adjustments that allow you to go where you want to go.

The trick, you see, is to stay on top of the flow. Whether you're in a canoe bouncing up and down the rapids, or a salesperson working through the day, the strategy is the same. You must stay in control of the flow.

Here are six strategies to help you.

I. Constantly reprioritize

Because your most detailed plans can often crack into a thousand pieces like a shattered window, you need to develop some disciplines to keep control of your day and turn decaying days into positive opportunities. One such discipline is to constantly check on your priorities throughout the course of the day, and to reprioritize as necessary.

Here's a technique that will serve you very well. Several times throughout the course of the day, ask yourself this question: "Am I doing the most effective thing I could be doing at this moment?" It's amazing how many times you will ask yourself that question, and answer it with, "No. I'm doing this stupid, unimportant thing. I should be doing something more effective."

For years, I had a negative, time-wasting habit. Whenever I had a bad sales call, I'd have to find a coffee shop and drink a cup of coffee or two, read the paper, and feel sorry for myself for a while before I ventured out to my next call. One day, after a bad call, as I was sitting in a coffee shop, I asked myself that question, "Am I doing the most effective thing I could be doing right now? No, I'm sitting in this coffee shop drinking coffee. I should be out making money." And off I went.

Create the discipline of asking yourself that question several times a day, and you'll dramatically improve your effective use of time..

Tips from the troops...

Managers, think carefully about requiring mandatory office time. If salespeople must come to the office, encourage them to come at the end of the day rather than the first thing in the morning. Office time is almost always the least productive portion of the workweek.

---

2. Stay close to the money

Okay, you have asked yourself the question, "Am I doing, right now, the most effective thing I could be doing?" And you suspect that the answer is no. But before you can be sure, you need to have some definition of effectiveness, some easy way to determine—of two or more choices—which is the most effective.

Or you may be faced with an impossibly long task or "to do" list. Shortly after you begin to keep a master list of things that you could or should or must do, you'll soon come to the point where you have too many to actually complete in the time you have. Some of them can be done later, some need to be done soon, and others aren't worth doing at all.

How do you sort this all out, and keep yourself focused on the most effective actions? Here's a guideline to help you sort it all out. Always do first that which is *closest to the money.*

Closest to the money means just that. Some tasks will result in dollars coming into the company before others will. When you are overwhelmed with too many tasks, apply the rule of *closest to the money* and do those first that will soonest bring you money.

Let's apply this to a typical situation and see how it works. You are in the middle of your day, and an appointment that you had planned for two hours ended in 15 minutes because your customer wasn't prepared for you. You are now sitting in your car, thinking, "What now?" You realize that you have these choices:

1. Pull over to a quiet place and work on that quote for Jones Brothers.

2. Cold call about 15 prospects and try to schedule appointments.

3. Try to see the engineer at Smith Brothers to confirm the specs for the new product, and carry them to purchasing to have them put into an RFQ.

4. Call my customer service rep and find out when the order will be delivered to White Manufacturing—then schedule a training seminar for them.

Which of these do you focus on first? Which are closest to the money? "Calling my customer service rep to find out when the order will be delivered to White Manufacturing and then schedule a training seminar for them" is closest to the money. The sooner you can get the order delivered, the sooner the bill will be paid. That's revenue into the company, and that's what we mean by *closest to the money*. As soon as the employees at White Manufacturering are comfortable with the new product and using it routinely, the sooner you can expect reorders.

"Trying to see the engineer at Smith Brothers to confirm the specs for the new product, and carrying them to purchasing to have them put into an RFQ" is second because it is likely to result in an order very soon. The order is closer to the money than the remaining three items.

Then, pulling over to a quiet place and working on that quote for Jones Brothers and cold calling about 15 prospects to schedule appointments are last, because they are furthest from the money. You haven't even seen these people yet, so the relationship is further away from turning into cash.

Closest to the money will keep you working at the most effective tasks, even in the midst of a turbulent and chaotic day.

> **When you are faced with a choice of multiple tasks, always choose that which is *closest to the money* to focus on first.**

3. Prepare to make good use of uncontrollable downtime

Uncontrollable downtime is that time that suddenly appears on your schedule because of things that happen outside of your control. You drive an hour for an appointment and discover that your customer called in sick that day and no one thought to call you. Now you have an hour or so of uncontrollable downtime.

Or you head out for a lunch meeting with a customer, and get a call on your cell phone, canceling the appointment. Another hour or so of uncontrollable downtime. Your well-planned day unravels around you.

Uncontrollable downtime happens regularly and unpredictably. You can either allow the uncontrollable downtime to disrupt your day by wasting the time away, or you can be prepared to make good use of it.

I learned about uncontrollable downtime the hard way. When I was selling surgical staplers, I often scrubbed with the surgeon who was learning to use the instruments. I was one of those people in caps, gloves, and mask, standing over the patient, across from the surgeon, in the operating room. When they were just learning to use the instruments, surgeons liked to have us nearby in case they had any problems with the staplers. Scrubbing for surgery was a necessary step to get the surgeon comfortable enough with the instruments to continue to use them.

Most of the surgical procedures in which the staplers were used were major bowel and gastric surgery, and those cases were usually scheduled, first thing in the morning, generally at 7 a.m.

I was working with a surgeon at a hospital about an hour's drive from my house. Since the surgery started at 7 a.m., I needed to get to the hospital at about 6:30 so that I could review the procedures and the instruments with the surgeon before scrubbing. That meant I had to leave my house around 5:15 a.m. But, because I always made it a practice to bring a box of donuts for the operating room nurses, I needed to leave at 4:45 to allow time to get to the donut shop. That meant getting up at 4 a.m.

One of the common practices in a major surgery is to postpone a case if the patient has a fever. The surgical team never wants to add any stress to the patient if the patient has some kind of infection.

You guessed it. Three days in row, as I stumbled into the OR suite at 6:30 a.m., having already been up for almost three hours, the OR Supervisor glanced at the surgical schedule, looked up at me, and said, "Oh, didn't anyone call you? The case has been postponed!"

On the third day, I decided that uncontrollable downtime was going to be an occupational hazard of my job and that, instead of becoming upset about it, I should take it in stride and be prepared for it.

Since then, I always carry some work to do with me wherever I go. That way, I do not become frustrated by uncontrollable downtime.

You can do the same. Always be prepared to make good use of uncontrollable downtime. That means always having something productive to do with you. That new product literature you need to study, your monthly expense report that needs to be completed, those quotes you have to write up, etc. A good selection of these kinds of projects, projects that may take 20 to 45 minutes each and can be worked into the course of your day, should always be in your briefcase.

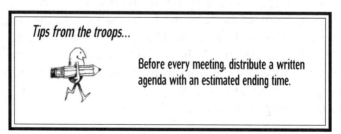

Tips from the troops...

Before every meeting, distribute a written agenda with an estimated ending time.

Use your weekly planning time to decide what projects you are going to take with you that week. That way, when you see the inevitable uncontrollable downtime appear, you'll be prepared to make good use of it.

Find a nearby library in which to work. Or look for a hotel lobby, a quiet coffee shop, or pull over in a mall parking lot and work in your car. You'll never waste uncontrollable downtime again.

4. Don't always immediately react

See if this sounds familiar: You have your day planned, and then you receive a phone call, fax, or e-mail from one of your customers with a problem for you to solve. The natural tendency is to drop everything and work on the problem. After all, isn't that good customer service?

But when you do that, you become reactive, and lose control of your day. So, isn't there some way to provide service but stay in control?

Yes. The problem is your assumption that just because someone calls, their problem is urgent and needs your immediate attention. Because you operate on that assumption, you immediately react. But that assumption isn't necessarily true. Often, the situation isn't really urgent, and you can address it later.

All you need to do is ask this simple question of your customer: "Can I take care of it...[fill in the most convenient time for you to do so]." Sometimes, your customer will say, "Sure, that's okay." On those occasions, you will have gained control of your day back again, and you can proceed with your plan.

Granted, sometimes it is an urgent issue. And on those occasions, you do need to take care of it as soon as you can. But if you ask the question, a good portion of the time you'll remain in control. By asking the question, you refuse to get caught up in immediate reaction.

5. Qualify and prioritize every opportunity

Here's a common scenario. You make the mistake of going into the office. A call comes in from someone you've never heard of before. The caller is in your territory, and is asking about one of your product lines. Customer service refers the call to you.

What do you do? Do you drop everything and respond to the prospect's request, even if it means your plans for the day get crumpled? Not necessarily. You apply the discipline of a smart sales time manager, and qualify the prospect first.

That means you need to ask some questions before you act. Find out:

◎ What prompts his/her interest in this product line?

◎ What time frame is he/she working with?

The first question, followed up with some more specific questions, can provide a great deal of information. You may discover that the caller is collecting information for next year's budget. Or that they have an urgent and immediate need. Those are two very different situations that should prompt two very different responses from you. If it's the first situation, you clearly have some time to respond when it is convenient for you. If it is the second, you may want to rearrange your schedule and see

Tips from the troops...

At the end of every meeting, summarize the action steps for every person. Saves time.

him immediately. The key is to ask some questions so that you can come to conclusions about the reality of their interest and the need for quick action on your part, if any.

Clearly, these two situations are only two of an unlimited number of possibilities. That's the point. It's not wise to drop everything and react to an opportunity without first qualifying it. Then, on the basis of your deeper understanding, you can make intelligent decisions.

6. Learn to say no

Salespeople love to be busy and feel needed. It's part of our typical personality. Because of that, we have a tendency to do everything asked of us. One of our customer service reps asks us to pick up a defective product at a customer's office, and we swing an hour out of the way to do so. The warehouse asks us to drop off an emergency shipment to a customer, and we waste an hour and half acting like a high-priced delivery service. A prospect calls and wants someone to talk to ASAP. You race out there without even qualifying the opportunity.

You can probably develop your own list of things you do because someone asks you. The problem is, it's really difficult to say no.

And as a result of our inherent disability to form the word no, we waste hours doing nonessential things.

The solution, of course, is to nurture our ability to say no, and to do so on a regular basis. Like any other difficult behavior, you probably need to make a strong commitment to this new behavior, and then practice it in order to become comfortable and competent.

Write out a commitment on a 3 x 5 card or self-sticky pad: *I will occasionally say NO.* Put that in a prominent place where you will see it regularly. Stick it to the screen on your laptop, or paste it across your cell phone.

Practice it a bit. Stand in front of the mirror and watch yourself say no. If you can't bring yourself to actually get the word out of your mouth, perhaps your spouse will help. He or she might model it for you. Perhaps they could say no, and then you could mimic them. With enough effort, I'm sure that the word no will come out of your mouth. Once you formulate it for the first time, you'll find it easier to say the next time.

With some disciplined practice, you may find that *no* becomes a regular part of your repertoire.

When that happens, you'll find yourself taking a major step forward in using your time effectively.

To implement this management secret:

1. Write out this question on a self-sticky pad and stick it where you will see it often. Imbed it into your screensaver, or set it up to pop up on your laptop: *Am I doing, right now, the most effective thing I could be doing?*

2. Do the same thing with the next question: *What's closest to the money?*

3. Do the same with this question: *Can I take care of it...?*

4. Make it a point to prepare for uncontrollable down-time every week.

5. Qualify and prioritize every opportunity.

6. Learn to say no.

The Sixth Time
Management Secret:

Clean Out
the Gunk!

Sometimes our problems with using time effectively are internal, silently lurking in the confines of subconscious routines. You can create the greatest plans in the world, have the best intentions, be full of energy and thoroughly prepared, but be rendered ineffective by mindless time-wasting habits, many of which you are probably not even aware.

Recently, I was interviewing salespeople for a project for one of my clients. One of the salespeople mentioned that he often obtained demonstration samples by coming into the office, visiting the warehouse, opening a box of the product he wanted to sell, taking one out, and re-closing the box.

As you can imagine, this gave the warehouse manager fits. However, there were more consequences to this practice than a furious warehouse manager. This is an example of salesperson's *gunk*!

What's gunk? Any practice that detracts from the time you spend with customers. In other words, unnecessary things that you do instead of meeting with customers. Usually, these are mindless habits that waste time—things you do routinely and rarely think about.

Most drainage pipes, over time, accumulate layers of gunk that clog up the system. The gunk accumulates silently and slowly until it eventually stops the flow of drainage completely.

Tips from the troops...

Stop checking your e-mail so often! Two or three times a day is enough. Any more frequently than that is an unnecessary interruption. Ditto for your voice mails.

Most salespeople accumulate layers of habit that erode the time you spend in front of the customer. It builds slowly and mindlessly, gradually accumulating to choke off the flow of positive efforts.

When we boil your job down to its essence, it is clear that the one thing your company wants of you—the one thing that you do that brings value to your organization, the essential reason for your job—is to interact with the customers. Everything else is a means to that end. So, in terms of priority, interaction with your customers and prospects is number one. Gunk is any practice on your part that reduces the time you spend with customers.

Salesperson's gunk

Samples

In the example above, not only did the salesperson detract from the purity of the inventory, cause needless stress for the warehouse manager, and potentially short ship a customer, he also spent time doing something that took him out of his territory. The hour or so he spent gathering samples was time that he could have spent making sales calls.

In a gunkless sales routine, you would call or e-mail the person who was responsible for maintaining samples, and ask for the appropriate sample to be sent. It should have taken 30 seconds to send an e-mail requesting a sample instead of an hour driving back and forth to the office to get it.

Sales literature

In a gunked-up system, you regularly drive into the office to collect the sales literature you need. In a gunkless system, you maintain literature inventories in your car or home office, and regularly replace your inventory by e-mailed or faxed requests.

Emergency shipments

I was recently scheduled to interview a number of salespeople for one of my clients. We had sessions scheduled every hour. One of the salespeople didn't make the appointment. The reason? He had to drive home, exchange cars with his wife, use the larger car to drive to the warehouse, pick up an emergency shipment, and deliver it to a customer.

While on one hand we can applaud the salesperson for taking care of the customer, on the other we need to recognize that this practice is an instance of extremely costly gunk.

This whole episode probably took the better part of a half-day of the salesperson's time. Not only was that a very expensive delivery, but the episode detracted from the salesperson's time and focus. Several sales calls were not made, and valuable face time with a customer did not happen, because the salesperson was acting as the company's highest paid delivery driver. The company could have hired a limousine service to deliver the product for less.

In a gunkless sales system, an inside person expedites back orders and arranges for emergency shipments so that you are free to concentrate on interacting with the customers.

Tips from the troops...

For the sales rep who works out of his or her home, everyday distractions can be a problem. Map out at least six hours a day for work activity, and don't let home and family interfere. Also, map out time for family and home, and don't let work interfere with that. Make sure everyone in your family knows and respects your schedule.

Office time

This is one of the largest contributors of sales system gunk. In a gunked-up system, salespeople come into the office regularly. Maybe you start every day there. That time in the office is generally your least productive time. There is coffee to drink, phone calls to take, mailboxes to empty, colleagues to talk with—all gunky practices that take up expensive selling time.

This is such a large issue that I have even developed a law similar in scope and dependability to Einstein's law of relativity. I call it Kahle's Law of Office Time. It states: *Whenever a salesperson has 30 minutes of work to do at the office, it will always take two hours to do it.* You know this to be true—an accurate observation of an immutable law of how the universe works. Whenever I've mentioned this law in my seminars, all the salespeople nod their heads in knowing affirmation.

This law has a huge impact on salespeople. Countless hours are lost every year in this specific glop of stinky gunk. In order to overcome it, you must strictly adhere to an important sub-commandment: *Stay out of the office!* Just don't go there. Arrange yourself and your files in such a way as to be able to operate completely free of the office.

Stay out of the office!

Keep your files at home. Store your samples in the garage. Create a workspace for yourself in the basement. Teach your kids to leave you alone when you are working there. Have the office forward your mail to your home. Ream this gunk out of your system!

I realize that this is an ideal that may be out of reach for many of you. Sometimes you must go into the office. The boss requires it. If you must go, then keep in mind the corollary to

Kahle's Law of Office Time. This states that if you go into the office at 8 a.m., with 30 minutes of work to do, you will not leave the office until 10 a.m. However, if you go into the office with that same 30 minutes of work to do, only you show up at 4:30 p.m., magically, you are done by 5 p.m.! So, apply sub-part A of the major rule:

Stay out of the office.
But, if you must go, go later in the day,
not first thing in the morning.

Not making appointments—just showing up unexpectedly

This is frequently listed as the number-one time-waster by attendees in my seminars. You know what often happens when you just show up—if you get any time with the customer at all, it is preoccupied, leftover time where good things rarely happen. If your customer sees you, he often resents your unexpected intrusion into his day. More frequently, he doesn't see you at all, and you've just wasted anywhere from 30 to 60 minutes, and made him a bit suspicious of you. Bad move. Call ahead.

Small talk with people in the office

Okay, a little of this is necessary to cement relationships. But is it really necessary that you review last weekend's football game one more time? Wouldn't your time be better spent talking with a customer?

Not planning your day

Shame on you. Reread the Second Time Management Secret.

Reading the morning paper

Early in my career as a consultant and sales trainer, I shared an office with a colleague who had come out of the banking industry. He began every day by spending the first hour reading *The Wall Street Journal*. It drove me crazy. No wonder checking account fees are so high. By the time he got to section two, I'd have 10 phone calls made and be bouncing out the door. I had to restrain myself from tearing the paper out of his hands and screaming at him, "Why don't you get to work!" Good thing he didn't report to me.

Taking long lunches

When I close a big deal or work especially hard at a sales training seminar or a big presentation, I'll sometimes treat myself to a long, leisurely lunch. I rationalize it by telling myself that I deserve a little R and R. Most days, however, I brown bag it. It takes less time, and I can use all the time that I can get my hands on. I don't have to find a place to eat, park the car, wait in line, wait to order, etc.

When I'm on the road making sales calls, I try to either have lunch with a customer, or use the lunch hour to drive from one appointment to the next. I'm a master at eating while driving.

Not trusting the system, double-checking everything

Trying to do everything yourself instead of relying on your support people

These two combine to create one of the biggest slugs of gunk around. It is an almost universal problem of which almost every salesperson is guilty to some degree. That includes you.

For each individual salesperson, it's a major time-robber. You know how it goes. You have to go into the office and write this order up yourself because your inside support staff just won't understand the details. They'll get it wrong. Or you can't trust your customer service person to expedite a special order, so you have to do it yourself. Or you better go into the office and get that sample because your sales administrator won't know exactly which one you need. Or you better meet the service technician at the customer's place of business to fully explain the situation to him, because otherwise, he's likely to get it wrong.

Any of this sound familiar? Of course it does. All of these are expressions of the attitude that you must do it yourself, because you cannot rely on other people in your organization to do it correctly, whatever "it" is.

Consider how many hours each month you spend exercising this noble attitude. It may cost you dozens of hours. It may even be the single most costly bit of gunk in your system. If you flush out this slug of gunk, you may be able to free up countless hours.

Where did this attitude come from? It's been my observation that most field salespeople have an "independent" mindset. They enjoy the freedom that comes with field sales. They like making decisions about how to spend their time and manage their days. Many have aspirations of being in business for themselves one day—independent businesspeople. Naturally, they tend to think that they have to do everything themselves. When

---

Tips from the troops...

Make efficient use of small amounts of time. For example, while waiting for your computer to log on to your e-mail account, read a page of a book or a magazine article.

some problem crops up, their natural response is to solve it themselves.

That may be a description of you. Now, it may be that at some time in the past, someone in the organization dropped the ball and did not complete some aspect of a project to your specifications. That's hardly enough evidence to warrant you jumping to the conclusion that you have to forever do it yourself. Especially in light of my observation that most of the time when someone inside the company doesn't do something as well as you could, it's because you have not fully explained the task, or you have not communicated as thoroughly as you should have. In other words, the problem was you, not them.

Suppose you were to reexamine all the tasks that you have, over the years, taken on yourself, when someone else in the organization could just as well be doing them. Checking on a back order and calling the customer to inform him of the status, for example. Make a list of all the possibilities. Consider every item on the list. How much time do you spend doing that thing yourself instead of trusting someone in the organization to do it? Next to each item on the list, put the number of hours per month you think you spend on that item. Use that number to prioritize your list, and pick one or two items on which to work. Later, when you have successfully dissolved those pieces of gunk, come back to the list and work on the next highest priority.

Now, take the one or two items you have identified as high priority, and think about how you can successfully turn them over to someone inside your company. It may be that there already is someone who is supposed to be doing them. The problem is you just don't trust them to do it correctly. Here's a question to ask yourself: "How can you change what you do in order to help them do that task more successfully?" Maybe you need to communicate more thoroughly what needs to be done. Maybe you need to set up a feedback system whereby they let you know when the task is successfully completed. Maybe you need to sit down with them and explain the way you would like to have it done. Maybe you have to apologize for your past rudeness to them. Maybe it's you!

You may want to bring your manager into this project. I'm sure he or she has a vested interest in seeing that you are operating as efficiently as possible. If some part of the system isn't working, then your manager needs to be aware of it. Enlist your manager's assistance. Sell him or her on the project. Show how many hours you can devote to selling if you can delegate those high priority tasks.

Regardless, make it a point to successfully delegate that task. It may take a few weeks to pull it off in a way that allows you to be comfortable. Focus on those one or two high-priority items and work methodically at turning them over.

When you've successfully done that, discipline yourself to keep it turned over. Remember, gunk accumulates silently and stealthily. It's easy to slip back into the mindset that you have to do it yourself. It's a natural response for most salespeople. But that mindset is one of your greatest time-wasters.

Other mindless habitual gunk

You probably have your own bad habits that inconspicuously crowd out your selling behavior. Here's a list I've compiled from my seminars. I've asked my seminar participants to reflect on their experiences, and identify some of these time-wasters; the following list contains those most frequently mentioned. I call them Frequently Practiced Mindless Gunk.

- ▣ Hand delivering paperwork to the office instead of mailing it in.

- ▣ Making personal calls on your cell phone.

- ▣ Using the office computer to surf the Internet.

- ▣ Taking long smoke breaks.

- ▣ Making personal calls on company time.

- ▣ Running personal errands on company time.

- ▣ Eating lunch by yourself instead of with a customer.

- ▣ Taking long coffee breaks.

- ▣ Being unorganized.

Got the idea? You may have a special little time waster that you've treasured for years. If you're going to be effective in our time-compressed age, now is the time to work to eliminate it.

The examples of gunk can go on and on. But you have the idea. Gunk is any habit or practice that detracts from you spending time in front of the customers.

From my experience, gunk is inevitable, and often invisible. Gunk habits develop with time and become part of the unwritten rules about how you do things. They become part of the mindless habits that occupy much of your day. Yet, they clog up your valuable time and energy.

One sure way to improve your productivity is to clean out the gunk, freeing your time and energy to devote to the essence of your job and the activity that will bring you revenue—interacting face-to-face with your customers.

Tips from the troops...

Block out 15-minute blocks of time and devote them to the tasks you need to do: prospecting, follow-ups, mailings, appointments, exercise, prayer, family, etc.

How to de-gunk your routines

I. Identify the gunk.

Write a detailed blow-by-blow description of how you spent a day. Or dictate it into a handheld recorder. Repeat a few times. Then review your list. Look for gunk. As an alternative, use the Gunk Getter self-assessment from our Sales Time Management Tool Kit (available at *salestimemanagement.com*).

Sometimes, gunk is so deeply ingrained in your habits and routines that you won't even recognize it. So, it may work better to have someone else review your notes.

Regardless, ask this question: *Are you doing anything that could, at least in theory, be done better or cheaper by someone else?* Anything that pops up as a response to that question is potential gunk. Then, when you have a list of a few gunky practices, prioritize them in order to work first on those that will give you the greatest improvement in sales time.

2. Decide to substitute some other action for any gunky practices you identified.

Remember that we're talking about habits here, and habits are hard to change. To give yourself the best chance of succeeding, don't try to just eliminate the gunk. Instead, try to substitute a positive action, and make that action a habit.

For example, let's say that your gunk analysis revealed that you have the habit of starting each day with a cup of coffee at the local coffee shop while you read the morning paper. Okay, that's clearly gunk. How do you get out of that habit? Not just by deciding to stop doing something, but rather by deciding to substitute something else more positive.

So, you decide to make your first appointment every day at 8:15, and to make your coffee at home and take it in a Thermos to drink as you drive.

You have now decided to substitute a positive action: 8:15 a.m. appointments, for a negative one: wasting time at the coffee shop.

3. Publicize your commitment.

You are much more likely to follow through on this change in habits if you publish your commitment. There is something about the pressure of telling someone else how you are doing that adds some energy to your effort.

Write down your commitment as specifically as possible. I call this creating a Precise Prescription. That's a prescription for your new behavior. The more precisely you write it, the more likely it is that you will follow through.

You could write down this statement, for example, *I'll make early morning appointments instead of stopping at the coffee shop.* That's a good intention, but it's not very precise. Suppose you rewrote to express it like this: *I wiil make an 8:15 a.m. appointment every day of the week.* That is more precise.

Notice that it is also measurable. Every day of the week is quantifiable. At the end of the week, you can look back and measure your performance. Did you accomplish your goal 100 percent of the time, 80 percent, etc? The more specific and measurable is your prescription, the easier you will find it to complete.

Now that you have it written down, let someone else know about it. Actually, the more people the better. Let your family know. Notify your boss. Tell a couple of colleagues about your plan. When you do this, you are setting yourself up for success. It is just more difficult not to do the new behavior when you know that several people are expecting that behavior from you. On the other hand, if you don't tell anyone, who is going to know if you blow it?

4. Monitor your progress.

Keep track of how you are doing. Each day, or at least once a week, review your progress and give yourself a rating. (See our Sales Time Management Tool Kit for a form to use.) When you reach the point that you are mindlessly doing this new behavior, that you don't have to think about it, you just do it. At that point, you will have created a habit. You won't have to monitor your performance anymore. You can go on to the next layer of gunk.

Preventing future gunk buildup

The unfortunate truth of the gunk in your drainage pipes is that as soon as you auger out the pipes, gunk will immediately begin accumulating silently. So it is with the gunk in your regular routines. You can never rest. Once you have successfully eliminated some gunky habit, be assured that you'll find another one lurking in the dregs underneath the first.

But take some comfort in this. Just as keeping the gunk from building up in your drainage pipes is easier than unplugging a stopped drain, preventing gunk from building up in your sales routines is easier than ridding yourself of habits that have been solidifying for years.

Tips from the troops...

Launch the new habit strongly.

Just as you use a small dose of drain cleaner as preventative maintenance to keep your pipes clean, so too you prevent gunk accumulation in your sales routines by using a small dose of the same processes you used to rid yourself of gunk.

1. Identify potential gunk.

Once a month, while you are doing your monthly planning (see the Second Management Secret), ask yourself, "Did I do anything this past month that, if repeated, could turn into gunk?" You may discover that you made a run to the office to pick up a sample when you didn't need to, or that you spent too much time enjoying a leisurely lunch.

2. Resolve to substitute some other behavior.

Right now, while it is on your mind and before you have an opportunity to repeat that gunky behavior, resolve to substitute some other tactic. For example, if you discover that you made an unnecessary run to the office for a sample, resolve right now to call and ask for the sample to be sent to you the next time you need one. Or if you discover that you spent too much time enjoying a leisurely lunch, resolve right now to make that 1 p.m. appointment 45 minutes away from your 11:30 a.m. meeting.

The time to prevent gunk buildup is now, before it has a chance to harden into an unconscious, time-wasting habit.

You'll need to be gunk vigilant for as long as you are in the business. Just like the pipes in your home need maintenance forever, so does the gunk in your routine.

To implement this management secret:

1. Analyze your current routine, identifying any gunk.

   - Write or dictate a detailed list of how you spent a few days, or

   - Use our "Gunk-Getter" from the Sales Time Management Tool Kit.

2. Prioritize those slugs of gunk that you want to work on first.

3. Write out "Precise Prescriptions" for your new gunk-less behavior.

4. Publish those prescriptions.

5. Substitute some positive behavior for the gunky practice.

6. Repeat and monitor it until it becomes a habit.

7. Move on to another slug of gunk.

The Seventh Time Management Secret:

Create Systems!

T here are some aspects of your job that you should approach this way: Think hard about how to do them most effectively and efficiently once, and then don't think about them again for a long time. When you think hard about the best way to do something, the outcome of that thinking is often a system. Creating effective systems for regular tasks is one of your key secrets.

The dictionary definition of the word *system* that comes closest to our application is this: *A regular, orderly way of doing something.*

Good systems bring you two powerful time management benefits. First, systems reduce the amount of time you spend on a task. That's efficient. Second, they allow you to wring the greatest value from that task. That's effective.

As an example, let's take something simple such as filling out an expense report form. Let's assume that your company requires you to complete a detailed expense report form and to send it each week, with all the supporting receipts, to the accounting office. One way to accomplish this is to be non-systematic. Stick those receipts in your pocket, in your planner, throw them in your suitcase, and lose them in your account folders. Then when you think about the form on Monday morning, and you realize it should have been mailed over the weekend, you can scrounge around the car, go through all your files, rummage through the pockets of the clothes you wore last week, and scrape together as many of them as you can find. Then you try to reconstruct the week's business expenditures, and rush to the mailbox to send this off. That will probably take at least an hour or so of good selling time, and result in a poor and inaccurate report, your manager nagging you, and the accounting office threatening to hold up your paycheck. Not a good move.

That's one approach to the task. On the other hand, you can choose to be systematic about it. You can decide, for example, that you'll keep a clipboard with the expense report attached to it on the front seat of your car. You'll get a resealable freezer bag and a stamped, addressed envelope, and clip them to the board. You'll resolve that every time you incur a business expense, you'll note it down immediately upon entering your car, and then you'll put the receipt in the freezer bag. Every Friday, on your way home, you total up the expense, put everything in the envelope, and mail it. Sunday evening, when you are preparing for next week, you open your supplies folder, take out another envelope and form, and clip it to the board so that that you are ready for the new week. Your task is complete, done accurately and on time, with minimum time on your part. At the next sales meeting, your manager praises you in front of the troops, and the accountant smiles as you walk by his office. Life is good.

The difference between the two ways of dealing with this task is that one was systematic, the other not.

There are lots of tasks that need to be done systematically. And that means that you need to create effective systems in order to accomplish them.

Tips from the troops...

A cluttered desk can be a major time-waster. Create a file folder, and fill it with all that you have to do that day or that week. On a sheet of paper in the front, prioritize those activities. Then work on one thing at a time, keeping everything not essential to that project off your desk.

Let's analyze the previous example in order to identify the parts of a system so that you replicate them for your purposes. Systems have these components:

- ▣ Outputs.

- ▣ Inputs.

- ▣ Processes.

- ▣ Tools.

- ▣ Disciplines.

Notice that the expense form system had a specific end result in mind—an accurate, complete form mailed on time. Systems always have outputs—results that they produce.

Systems also have inputs—things that go into the process. In this case, the inputs were the notations of money spent and the receipts that documented those expenditures.

Systems have processes—step-by-step methods of completing the task. These processes are the heart of any system. Without well-defined processes, the system is ineffective.

I'm a great believer in processes. Much of my work as a consultant is to help my clients create and improve their processes. Good processes are at the very core of good work.

In this expense form example, the process was this:

1. Note the expense on the form immediately upon entering the car following an expenditure.

2. Put the receipt in the freezer bag.

3. Total the amounts and mail the report every Friday afternoon on the way home.

4. Sunday evening, replenish the supply.

Good systems have good tools. Tools are the things you use to help you accomplish the processes. In this case, the tools were the clipboard, the freezer bag, the forms, and the stamped envelope.

Finally, systems have disciplines. This means that the people involved in the system have the personal discipline to use it the way it was designed. In this case, the person is you! It won't do any good to design a slick system if you don't bother to consistently work that system. That's called discipline.

If you are going to be a smart time manager, you need to create and implement systems for some routine tasks—anything that you do over and over again. These can be relatively minor, paper-workish kinds of tasks like expense reports, call reports, creating proposals, etc. Or they can be major parts of your job, like preparing a presentation, cold-calling prospects, and so on. Here's a list of the typical kinds of tasks that often benefit from a systematic approach:

- ▣ Making appointments.

- ▣ Keeping track of progress in each individual account.

- ▣ Collecting good information about their customers.

- ▣ Managing information about products.

- ▣ Collecting information about competitors.

- ▣ Preparing quotations.

In every case, you need to spend some up-front time thinking hard about your system to accomplish this task, creating and implementing a process and tools to handle the inputs and outputs. Once you have your system in place, then you need to follow it with discipline so that you can reduce the amount of time you spend on it and increase the results.

There are some special aspects of your job that need particular attention. We're going to look closely at these.

Managing information

The average salesperson could spend 10 to 12 hours a week doing nothing but dealing with information. When I make that statement in my seminars, everyone nods their heads in agreement. There are computer reports to review, accounts receivable records to consider, new price lists, service bulletins, new product information, software upgrades, as well as hundreds of e-mails, faxes and memos!

If you don't gain control of the quantity of information coming your way, you'll be overwhelmed and rendered ineffective. Once you have protected yourself from being swept away by the tidal wave of useless information, you had better create some systems to make sure that you are collecting, storing, and using good information. This is, after all, the Information Age.

Let's focus on two aspects of information management: defense and offense.

Defense

Technological advances in recent years have multiplied the amount of information that you must handle. The quantity of information landing on your lap has increased from sources all around you. Think about how much information you must keep about your customers. A few years ago, it was okay to keep everything in your head. Today, you need forms, documents, files, and systems, both electronic and paper, to keep it all straight. Consider the technical details of the products and programs you sell. Aren't they more complex and sophisticated than just a few years ago? And all that complexity takes the form of additional information that you must organize and master.

What about the computer systems you use and the information produced by them? Most salespeople I know could spend eight to 12 hours a week just reviewing computer printouts if they choose to. Add in memos from the boss, service bulletins, price increases, government regulations, new product specifications, the details of more complicated applications, and your job is awash in information. And that's before your spouse gives you a grocery list to pick up on the way home.

The sheer volume of information coming at you is like an approaching tidal wave. If you don't create some safe haven for yourself, you're going to be rendered ineffective by the absolute mass of information.

Imagine how many precious selling hours you could waste each week if you don't harness that tidal wave of information. Or imagine the time robbed from your family and personal life by the time it takes to handle more and more stuff.

It's time to recognize the problem for what it is—a serious and malevolent new threat to your effectiveness.

So, what do you do? How do you overcome this threat? How do you get control over the flow of information and protect your valuable selling time?

One strategy is to become defensive. I don't mean that you deny any responsibility for your own actions and you blame everybody else for your problems. What I do mean is that you develop ways to defend yourself from being overcome with useless information. The idea is to keep information that is tempting but useless from stealing your time.

To do so, you need to understand and implement two key processes. The first is *screening*. Imagine the screen on your window. This fine mesh allows those breezes that you want to flow into the house, while it keeps out those insects that you don't want. That's the idea behind the process of screening—allowing in that which you want, and keeping out that which you don't want. Unfortunately, you can't surround yourself with a physical screen. But you can implement the discipline of "screening" all the information that comes your way. To do so, you need to establish the habit of quickly assessing every piece of information that cries out for your time and to quickly decide if it is likely to be useful. *Useful* is the key word.

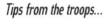

Tips from the troops...

Eliminate sales reports. But first, get you boss's blessing.

If your quick perusal of a piece of information leads you to believe that it may be useful, you let that piece in. If you believe it will not be useful, you keep it out. In other words, you dispose of it.

Let's imagine a scenario. You've come into the office and pulled a pile of stuff out of your mailbox. The first thing you see is a new price list for a product line you rarely sell. Is this useful to you? Probably not. You throw it out. Next is a service bulletin on a piece of equipment that you haven't sold in years. Is it useful? Probably not. Out it goes. Next is a computer report comparing last year's sales in three product lines to the sales from two years ago on those same lines. Is it useful? In the round file it goes.

Finally, there's a memo from the boss outlining the agenda, location, and schedules of sales meetings for the next two months. Better hold on to that one. You continue on this way, quickly appraising every piece of information, and disposing of every piece you deem to be not *useful*.

This whole process may have only taken a few seconds. But your disciplined screening process kept a lot of useless information from sucking away your time. The net effect was that you created more selling time for yourself by disciplining yourself to keep out that which is useless, and to allow in that which is useful. I'm using paper snail mail as an example, but you can use the same concept and tools with e-mail and phone messages.

Now you have a pile of stuff that, on first glance, looked like it might be useful. Now what do you do? Implement the second key process—*triaging.* You may be familiar with the word. It has a medical origin. In every hospital emergency room, there is someone who performs the triaging function. They make a quick assessment of the condition of the incoming patients, and then send them to different degrees and types of treatment depending on that initial assessment. One person is told to wait in the waiting room for a while longer, another is sent directly to the OB department, and another is admitted to surgery.

The person who does the triaging sends each patient to a location for treatment based on that initial assessment.

You employ a similar process when you confront the useful pile on your desk. You look at each piece of information, and send it to the location where it can be dealt with appropriately. For example, you have a spot for *read and handle immediately.* You have a file for *put this stuff into my account folders.* You have a folder for *study this when you have time.* You have yet another marked *file with product information.*

Now that you know what your options are, you are ready to triage the pile of information on your desk. Look at each piece, and place it in the location where you can deal with it appropriately. If you have thought about this before and arranged an effective file system, this process may take you a just a few moments. At the end of that time, you have everything in its place and you can now deal with it in the time and place you choose. You sit down with the *read and handle immediately* pile and process that. The *study this when you have time* file goes in your briefcase to be reviewed while you are waiting for appointments, or on those occasions when you are having lunch by yourself. The stuff for account folders and product folders goes home with you and is reviewed and filed in your home office all at once on Friday afternoons or Saturday mornings.

By implementing these two disciplines, you've taken what could have been an hour or two of information-engagement and turned it into a few moments of disciplined involvement on your part. You've gotten back hours of selling time, and not allowed the tidal wave of information to wash you away.

The process of screening and triaging can work for you with any kind of information. Apply it to your list of daily e-mails and e-mail attachments. Ditto the stuff in your inbox, and the pile of envelopes and catalogues that appear every day in the mail. Likewise for phone messages. Do the same with your choice of Internet surfing and TV-channel hopping. Immediately discard the useless and then triage the useful.

Let's apply our systems thinking to this task. The objective of your defensive information management system is to efficiently handle the appropriate information as quickly as possible. The input is composed of all the bits and pieces of information coming your way. The output is the useful information, appropriately arranged. The key processes are screening and triaging, and the tools are your triaging files and your useful criteria. All that's lacking is your discipline to follow the system.

Offense

It's not enough to protect yourself from the onslaught of useless information. You must also be sure that you are acquiring the appropriate amount of useful information. This is the

Information Age, and you need to equip yourself with the right kinds and amounts of information. Remember, sales is a thinking person's game. You can't think well if you don't have the raw material. And raw material is information. Good information enables you to make good decisions. Poor or spotty information leaves you at a competitive disadvantage. You can't make a good decision about which hotel to vacation at if you don't know anything about your options. You can't make a decision about which customer will most likely be interested in your hot new product unless you have some information about your customers.

There was a time when you could keep all that kind of information in your head. No need to write anything down—you'd remember it. Of course, that was when you were younger and could remember it. Not only that, but things were a lot simpler then. Today, simple is not a word I'd use to describe any part of sales.

If you are going to be a successful salesperson in the 21st century, you must be a smart time manager, and that means you need to be adept at systematically acquiring good information. That includes information about:

- Your customers and prospects.

- Your products and services.

- Your competitors.

- Your programs and deals.

Your system should address the issues of *collecting the information that will be most useful to you, storing it adequately, and using it regularly.*

Because our world is constantly producing new information, your system isn't the kind of thing you do once and forget. Rather, it has to be a dynamic system that is constantly processing, sorting, storing, and accessing new information.

Let's look at each of these categories consider how we could create a system to collect, store, and use that information.

Customers and prospects

Ask yourself what kinds of information would be *ideal* for you to have. What, ideally, would you like to know about your customers and prospects? I would suggest, at a minimum, that you need to have an account profile form for each individual decision-maker as well as one for each account.

Account profile form

An account profile form is full of questions, and spaces for the answers to questions. The questions are all about one of your accounts, or one of the individuals within that account. The form is the document on which you store that useful information.

You may be using a well-designed contact management piece of software. If so, the software probably requires an account profile of you. The profile is usually the first couple of screens in the customer master file. Some of these software programs are available off the shelf; others have been customized or created by your company.

If you are not using an appropriate piece of software with a thorough account profile built into it, then you need to create one on your own.

A well-designed, systematically executed account profile form can be one of your most powerful strategies for acquiring a competitive edge, because it provides you a way to collect quantitative information that will allow you to know your customers more thoroughly than your competition. For example, you can have spaces for information about the account's total volume of the kind of products you sell, the dates of contracts that are coming up, the people from whom they are currently buying, and so forth. All of that seems pretty basic. However, most salespeople have no systematic way of collecting and storing that information. While you may occasionally ask a certain customer for parts of it, you probably aren't asking every one of your customers for all the information. And you're probably not collecting it, storing it, and referring to it in a systematic, disciplined way.

Do you think your competitors know exactly how much potential each of their accounts has? Do you think they know how many pieces of production equipment each customer has, and the manufacturer and year of purchase of each? Probably not.

If you collect good quantitative marketing information, you'll be better equipped to make strategic sales decisions. For example, you'll know exactly who to talk to when the new piece of equipment from ABC manufacturer is finally introduced. You'll know who is really ripe for some new cost-saving product that's coming, or the new program your company is putting together.

In addition to the quantitative information, the form provides a system for collecting personal information about the key decision-makers. Once you have a place for "hobbies" and "organizations belonged to," you'll have to collect that information and fill in the space. Now imagine getting ready for the next sales call on that customer and reviewing the things that

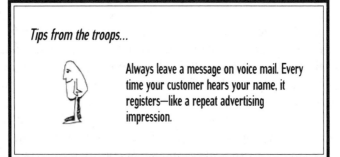

Tips from the troops...

Always leave a message on voice mail. Every time your customer hears your name, it registers—like a repeat advertising impression.

he likes to talk about, refreshing your memory on the name of his spouse, and the names and schools of each of his kids. Do you think you'll be better prepared to have an enjoyable, relationship-building conversation with that customer than your competitor will? Of course you will.

The act of asking the questions prompted by the form also creates a process of deeper communication between you and your customer. You'll talk about deeper things and more personal things than most of your competitors. Your customer perceives your inquiries as sincere interest (which they are) and responds to you accordingly.

Finally, the form allows you to store important information someplace other than in your head. The problem with keeping information just in your head is that it isn't always readily accessible. When you want to have a relaxed conversation with one of your customers about his interests, you can't always remember than he golfs and was a starting halfback on his college football team. However, if you have that information stored on a form, you can review it just before you go in to see your customer, and put it uppermost in your mind.

To some degree, every good salesperson implements these concepts. The difference between the run-of-the-mill salesperson and the master, however, is the degree to which the master disciplines himself to stick to a systematic approach. Most salespeople do it as they think of it, but don't keep the information systematically. Masters understand the need to discipline themselves, and thus do a more thorough job of collecting information.

Have I sold you on the need to use an account profile form? Good. As you begin to implement this idea, think in terms of two types of forms. The first captures the account information— size, number of employees, etc. The second focuses on the individual decision-makers within that account, and contains personal information—like hobbies, outside interests, etc.

You should have one account form for every account, and as many personal profiles as there are key contact people within that account.

It may be that you are working with contact-management software and your company has already designed an electronic version of these forms. Great. Use it consistently and skip the next section.

However, even at this date, less than half of the salespeople in this world are automated. Chances are, then, that either you are using a personal information manager like Act or Outlook on your own, or that you are still using paper files. It's time to become more systematic about using your account profiles.

Contact log

The next information collection and storage tool is a contact log. It's just a simple record of what you talked about in each visit, and what your plan is at that point. It sounds simple, and it is.

But again, many salespeople don't discipline themselves to systematically collect and store this information. Instead, they rely on their memory. I don't know about you, but I know that if I make several sales calls during the course of a day, by the end of the day, I've forgotten half of everything I talked about. If I don't write it down immediately after the call, I lose it.

The contact log can take several forms. When I began my sales career, I preferred to use 3 x 5 cards. They were small and inconspicuous, they could be easily kept in my breast pocket wallet or planner, and they were readily available. After each call, I'd simply write down what happened, and what I needed to do next. When a card was filled up, I'd number it and file it in the account folder. That way, I could review years' worth of sales calls to see the history of a contract or piece of business.

If you prefer, use a legal pad or simple 8 1/2 x 11 lined pages. Or if you're automated, you can use a laptop computer or palm device to collect and store the same information.

Regardless of the technology you decide to use, the important thing is that you make a systematic and disciplined effort to record your contacts.

Account files

One last information management tool to help you with your prospects and customers is your set of account files. Create a set of manila folders or pocket files for each of your accounts. You'll probably need at least two files for each account. In one, keep all historically important information. For example, keep copies of all the quotes you've made to that account and, on each, note who got the business, when it may come up again, and your best understanding of why someone else was awarded the business. Any other notes that you've made regarding competitors, or other helpful information about the account, should go into the historical file.

The other file is your working file. This is the one you take with you to the account. Keep your profiles, contact logs, and current quotes and proposals in there.

Tips from the troops...

Make an appointment for the first and last calls of the day. That keeps you in the field all day, and helps overcome the temptation to cut the day short.

You may also use it to carry pieces of literature you intend to leave with your account, as well as any helpful pieces of information that you may need while you're on the sales call.

When you have this filing system in place, you've organized the most important part of your job—the information about your customers and prospects. Now let's take a look at the other major aspects of your information system.

Competitor files

Set up manila folders for each of your main competitors. If your territory overlaps with several reps from the same competitor, you may need to have a folder for each of those reps.

Your job now is to collect bits and pieces of information, to compile them, and then to study them to see if they reveal any trends.

Start by collecting information in a disciplined way. Anytime you collect a piece of information about a competitor, file it in the appropriate file. When you lose a piece of business to a competitor, note what products were lost, when, and by how much. When you see some evidence of that competitor promoting a certain product line to one of your accounts, store that information. Collect every little bit of information you can.

In time, you'll have collected a powerful bank of useful information. Every now and then, open the file and review your bits and pieces of information. Study what you have there. It's amazing how often you'll discover trends and patterns in the way competitors operate. And if you can uncover some patterns, you'll be able to predict their behavior in the future.

Refer to it regularly. You'll find it particularly helpful in a big, competitive bid when you're trying to figure out what everyone else is going to do.

Tickler files

A tickler file is just a convenient way to jog your memory when there is something you need to do. Again, if you're automated, your contact manager will automatically do this for you.

If you're not automated, then you need to set up a system. Here's an easy way to do so. Get a file that holds 3 x 5 cards, and set up indexes with labels for every month from January through December, and another set with labels numbered one through 31. Then, when you want to be reminded to do something, write it on a 3 x 5 card, and put it under the appropriate month you need to be reminded to take action.

Let's say you present a new product line to one of your accounts. Your contact says that it's currently under contract, but he'd be willing to consider an evaluation of your product line in June. Simply put a little note to talk to that account about the new product line on a 3 x 5 card, and file it in the June section. On the first of June, take every card out of the June file, and place it in the number file that corresponds to the date that you want to talk to your account about it. Do this with each card in the monthly section every month. Then, each day, review the things you need to do. It's a simple way to keep organized and makes sure that nothing slips through the cracks.

Product files

You need to keep information about the products and services that you sell. Some of you are thinking, "I don't need to have that, it's all at the office." The problem with that is that you must go to the office to get it. And every time you go to the office, you waste precious selling time.

I recommend that you keep a separate, duplicate set of files at your home. These files should contain two sets of information. The first file is a reference file with technical details, competitors' products, and so on, which you may need to study from time to time.

The second file should contain the literature that you'll need to hand out.

Other files

Internal communications

From time to time you'll need to create, process, or keep paperwork for someone inside your business. Create a couple of files for that eventuality—perhaps one for customer service, another for purchasing or inventory control, and one for your boss.

General learning

The need to continue to improve in your job means that you'll need to dedicate time to the task of learning. When you see a good article about sales skills, relationship building, or perhaps some aspect of an application of your products, put it into your learning file, and review it when you set time aside to do so.

When you have completed the organization of your file system, you've created most of the tools you need to implement an information management system.

You've taken this major task of managing information and turned it into a system.

The *objective* is to supply yourself with a sufficient quantity of useful and accessible information. The inputs are the pieces of information you collect methodically as part of your job. The outputs are the useful observations, and insights you make as you use this information to gain tactical and strategic advantage. The processes are the questions you ask to collect the information, the methods you use to store it, and the procedures you follow when you access and use it. The tools are the hard-copy files and electronic devices you use to manage your system.

Creating and effectively using such a system is one of the marks of a master salesperson. Our information-rich age brings with it a strong temptation to wallow in information. Without a system to manage information, the sheer quantity of that information will overcome you.

You can review product literature for hours every day. You can study last week's sales reports and credit memos, review the details of a sales promotion, revisit the last 10 sales calls you made to an account, all while you channel surf around 40 TV stations or cruise the Internet.

Tips from the troops...

Use commuting time to listen to motivational or educational messages. You'll stay motivated and have more energy.

The trick is to create a system that allows you to handle the flood of information, and then to operate the system with discipline. The more quickly you handle information, the more hours you'll have to devote to selling.

Systems thinking

Remember that the issue here is to take those routine tasks and create a system to address them. The system will allow you to do two things:

1. Handle the task as efficiently as possible.

2. Wring the most value from the task as possible.

As you address your system, think about:

1. What your objectives are.

2. What the input is.

3. What the output should be.

4. What processes to use.

5. What tools will help you.

Think hard about your system at first, and then review and refine it occasionally. In doing this, you'll take a major step forward in being both effective as well as efficient.

To implement this management secret:

1. Make a list of all the routine tasks that you could conceivably systematize.

2. Identify the one task that has the greatest potential to make you more effective or efficient.

3. Use the components of a system as a template to create a system to manage that task:

   - Outputs.

   - Inputs.

   - Processes.

- Tools.
- Disciplines.

4. Pay specific attention to your systems for managing information.

5. Create your triaging files and implement the defensive information management system.

6. Create your other files, and implement the offensive information management system.

7. See our Sales Time Management Tool Kit for tools to help you do all this.

The Eighth Time
Management Secret:

Stick to an
Effective
Sales Process!

In the last chapter, we looked at the importance of being systematic in your approach to the repetitive tasks that you must perform. In this chapter, we're taking the same approach to the major task that you face—the Big One.

And you're wondering, "What's the *Big One*?" It's selling. In other words, the big task, the reason your company hired you, the value you bring to your company, the heart of the sales job, is this—influencing your customers to purchase your products and services.

That's it. All the other things are peripheral to this one task. It is the essence of your job. And if you are systematic about accomplishing this major task, you'll take great leaps forward in your effectiveness and efficiency. You'll become a superstar of time management, and a producer of extraordinary results.

Too many salespeople are haphazard and unstructured in their approach to selling. They have no process they follow, no model by which to understand and organize their efforts. Their sales calls are only minimally planned, if at all. Their strategy in an account is limited to thinking about their next sales call. As a result, their efforts are often unfocused, and they waste tremendous amounts of their time as well as their customers' time.

The key is to have a clear model of how you go about selling, and then to fit all of your efforts into this model. In a moment, I'll share with you my model—the Target System. First, let's consider some of the benefits of using this approach to your major responsibility.

Tips from the troops...

Get adept with technology. Use a laptop with some form of contact manager to collect and use information about your customers and prospects.

Benefits to using a sales process model

A well-defined effective sales process provides you a way to think about each customer and prospect, and put your efforts into a context. Sales calls aren't made just to make them. Rather, you see every sales call as a step forward in the process. So you have a specific objective in mind for each sales call, and an overall strategy for every account and every opportunity within each account.

Your adherence to a sales process, then, keeps you focused on the most important outcomes (your sales call objectives) for the most important interactions (your face-to-face sales calls) of the most important part of your job (your relationships with your customers). This powerful tool prevents you from squandering time and effort.

The Target System

This is called the Target system after one of the visual images I use to illustrate some of the key aspects of the process.

Let's first look at the whole process, then, briefly describe each of the steps to the process. Here's a diagram of the process:

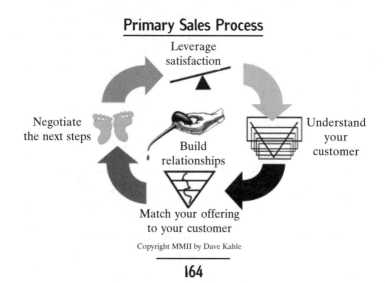

Primary Sales Process

Leverage satisfaction

Negotiate the next steps

Build relationships

Understand your customer

Match your offering to your customer

Copyright MMII by Dave Kahle

I. Build relationships.

This step of the process is illustrated by the oilcan. The idea is that the relationships you create with your customers lubricate the rest of the process, making everything else easier. It is possible for you to sell without great relationships with your customers. It's just extremely difficult. If your customers know you, trust you, and are comfortable with you, it makes everything else much easier. It's like oiling the gears in a machine. It might work without it, but the oil makes everything move more easily.

The oilcan is pictured in the center of the process because it is central to all you do, with its positive impact spreading to every phase of the sales process, every interaction, and every task associated with it. Further, building relationships is not an event that you complete in a sequential fashion. It is a part of every step in the process.

It's something you do in every sales call, during every phone call, with every e-mail. Relationships are at the heart of selling.

2. Peel the onion—understand your customer.

Suppose you've just come back from your company's annual sales meeting. For three days, you sat in meetings and ate hotel food. Now you're home, and you'd like nothing more than a cold drink and a home-cooked meal. You suggest a big salad for dinner, and your spouse agrees, suggesting that you peel the onion.

You get out a big, fat Bermuda onion, one of those that are about the size of a softball. You position it carefully on a cutting board, and root through the drawer until you find a sharp meat cleaver. Steadying the onion with one hand, you raise the meat cleaver above your head, and, with a karate-type movement, smash the meat cleaver neatly into the center of the onion, splitting it evenly in two.

You pick up one of the onion halves and examine it from the inside. You note that it has layers and layers, each deeper and more tightly compressed than the one surrounding it. You begin to peel the onion, stripping off the skin. As you pull off the skin of the onion, you notice that the skin is thin, dry, and crispy, with very little scent. However, as you peel each layer, one at a time, you soon come to the conclusion that each layer is more strongly scented than the one above it, and that the strength of the onion's pungency comes from the inside out.

That's the best way to understand this next step in the process. The real beginning to the sales process is working to achieve an understanding of what your customer wants and needs. When you have that understanding, you can move to the next step of the process, which is matching your products or services to those needs.

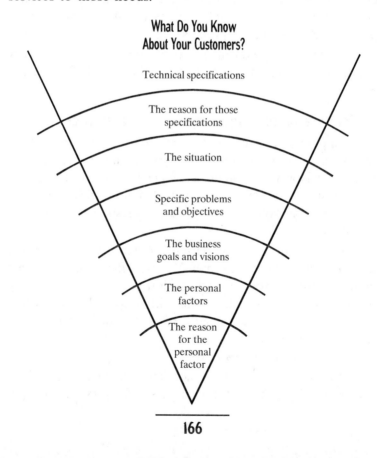

What Do You Know About Your Customers?

Technical specifications

The reason for those specifications

The situation

Specific problems and objectives

The business goals and visions

The personal factors

The reason for the personal factor

Just like there are layers and layers to an onion, there are layers and layers to your customer. Just like the superficial layers of an onion are thin and mild, the superficial levels of your customers have little strength. But as you peel the onion deeper and deeper, the strength increases. So, too, with you customer.

Let's apply this specifically to understanding your customer in a sales situation. Look at the illustration. Imagine it to be a slice of that onion. On the very surface are the technical specifications for the product or service the customer wants. For example, let's say you call on one of your customers and he says, "I need to purchase three green metal widgets that are 1/2 x 6 inches." Many salespeople would say, "Okay, they are $2.50 each." In this example, the salesperson understood the customer at the most superficial level—technical specifications— and responded in kind.

But you can go deeper in understanding the customer by discovering the reason behind those specifications.

Our rep, when confronted with the same request, may say, "What are you going to use them for?" or, "Is there a reason you asked for metal instead of plastic?" This kind of response will uncover the next level, the *reason* for the specifications.

There's more. *Situation* refers to the history behind the need, and the circumstances surrounding the need. For example, let's say that our salesperson now replies, "John, what's your situation? Why is this an issue now?" When the customer replies to that question, he has uncovered a deeper layer of need.

Yet you're still pretty close to the surface. When you uncover the specific problems and objectives under the original request, you deepen your understanding of the customer. Suppose your customer says, "We're having a problem with our second shift production. The line keeps breaking down. Our maintenance supervisor wants to stockpile some of the parts that he has been regularly replacing."

Now you have an understanding of the specific problems and objectives. There is more. Suppose you ask how that problem affects the rest of the company. And suppose your customer explains the effect of the breakdown on production, net profits, and overtime pay for the second shift. Now you understand the customer on an even deeper level.

But you can go deeper still. When you ask how those systematic problems affect his business goals, and you learn that it's particularly troublesome because your customer's goals are to increase net profits by 5 percent this year, you understand the customer at an even deeper level.

You take a significant plunge deeper when you are able to understand how the situation affects the individual with whom you're talking. For example, when you know him well enough to ask, "John, how can I make you look good in this transaction?" and get an honest response, you've penetrated to a new layer of understanding.

Finally, when you understand the individual motivations— the reasons for the personal factors—you understand customers at levels that few salespeople ever approach. That's where the masters work. Those motivations are often emotionally driven. So, when you understand the customers' emotions— how the situation makes them feel, you've arrived at the heart of the onion.

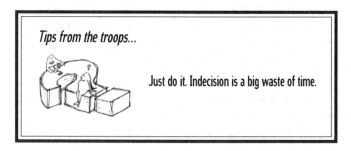

Tips from the troops...

Just do it. Indecision is a big waste of time.

3. Match your products and services to the customer's needs.

Once you have achieved a deep and detailed understanding of the customer's needs and interests, the next step is to select and present to the customer your solution—matching your best combination of products and services to his/her needs. Not only do you select and create the best match, in addition, when you present it, you show how your solution matches the customer's needs.

Let's say, for example, that you sell a variety of computers, peripherals, and network hardware. Your customer has indicated a need to upgrade several pieces of the system in his customer service call center. When you peeled the onion, you discovered that the call center was being repositioned, strategically, to take over more and more of the detail work that the outside sales force formerly did.

Every other competitor will bring in a bid on equipment. But because you peeled the onion, your proposal shows the customer how they can use your system to continually grow the number and sophistication of the tasks they perform, so that the customer service center will have the computing power to meet their strategic objectives.

Instead of just quoting a price on equipment, you matched your solution to the customer's deeper needs. Good job. That will distance you from your competitors and make your time spent with this customer more effective.

4. Negotiate the next step.

Assume that you have done a thorough job of matching your solution to the customer's needs. If so, then it is reasonable to expect that the customer should do something about it. Perhaps he asks for a demonstration or evaluation of your piece of equipment, or some more information, or agrees to take it to the committee, or present it to the boss, or buy it now.

Regardless, in every selling process, sooner or later it comes down to the customer agreeing to do something, to take some action as a result of your work. When you gain an agreement with the customer on what exactly that next step is, and a commitment is made to implement that action, you have achieved this step in the process.

5. Leverage satisfaction.

Sooner or later, someone is going to buy something from you. After they have made that decision, and after the product or service has been delivered and used by the customer, then comes the last step in the process. Many salespeople never follow through on what is one of the most powerful sales calls they can make—the follow-up call.

By assuring satisfaction, getting the customer to say, "Yes, it is working well," or "Yes, it was a good decision," you open the door for additional opportunities. You leverage that satisfaction to other opportunities either inside or outside of the company. If there is no immediate opportunity within the company to expand your sales and sell more, then you ask for referrals to others who might buy your stuff.

If there is an opportunity to sell more to this customer, then this is the best time to begin that process by discussing that opportunity. And when you have that discussion, guess what? You are back at the "peeling the onion" step of the process with the customer, moving through the sales process again.

Using the sales process as a time management tool

The Target System is a basic selling system designed to be customized to each company's unique situation. You may have a process that is considerably more complex than that. I once worked with a client where we designed a 27-step selling process. Regardless of what process you use, the important thing is that you use an effective, reproducible process. This process can become one of your most effective time management tools, because it keeps you focused. Here's a way to start making use of it. Create a matrix that looks something like this:

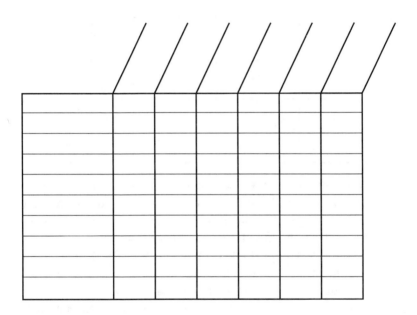

For a new product or service introduction

Now, suppose that you have a new product line (Red Widgets) that you want to sell in each of your 10 key accounts. Note *Red Widgets* at the top, list the 10 accounts down the left column, and then note each step of the sales process in the angled slots on the top. Your matrix now looks like this:

Relationship with Key People	Understand the Customer's Need (Peeled the Onion)	Presented Our Match	Negotiated the Next Step	Deal!	Follow Up to Leverage Satisfaction

Use this in your weekly or monthly planning to assess what progress you have made, and to focus you on the next step. For example, let's say that you called on Jones Manufacturing, had lunch with the senior buyer, and discovered that widgets are very important to them. They use $200,000-worth a year, but they are under contract with a competitor for widgets through June of next year. The buyer suggests you introduce the new widget to John Jones, the production engineer, sometime around January.

When you review your notes that afternoon, you note that, as it applies to widgets, you haven't yet built a relationship with the production engineer. In fact, you don't know him. And in spite of the information you got from the senior buyer, you really don't know what they are looking for in a widget, how it fits into their system, etc. You haven't yet peeled the onion in any but the most superficial way. As it relates to Jones, you haven't even accomplished step one in the sales process. What's the next step? Meet and create a relationship with John Jones.

You also called on Smith Brothers. It's a much smaller organization, and you know everyone, including the owner/CEO. He sees you, and likes your new red widget. You learn how many widgets they use, what problems they've had with widgets in the past, why they use the brand they do, how they use them, and what they are currently paying for them from a competitor. What's your next step in the process? You already have a relationship, you've peeled the onion regarding widgets, and you've shown him your widget. What now? Negotiate the next step. You propose a trial evaluation, and he agrees. You set up a date and send an e-mail to your customer service teammate with the details, and ask that he order the necessary supplies.

That evening, your matrix looks like this:

	Relationship with Key People	Understand the Customer's Need (Peeled the Onion)	Presented Our Match	Negotiated the Next Step	Deal!	Follow Up to Leverage Satisfaction
Jones						
Smith	✓	✓	✓			

Your use of a sales process has kept you on track, focused you on moving the projects forward, and given you a specific next step. It saves you time and helps you become more effective.

Multiple projects in a single customer

Here's another way to use the sales process to organize and focus your sales time. Let's say you sell multiple products or services to your customers. You can use the sales process and the matrix as a way of staying on top of all those projects. Here's an example. One of your key accounts is Ajax Inc. You have 10 product lines that Ajax can buy from you. So, you set up your matrix with Ajax as the subject, the steps to the sales process in the slots along the top, and each of the 10 product lines in the left-hand column, so that it looks like the following:

AJAX	Relationship with Key People	Understand the Customer's Need (Peeled the Onion)	Presented Our Match	Negotiated the Next Step	Deal!	Follow Up to Leverage Satisfaction
Widgets						
Red Widgets						
Green Widgets						
DoDods						
Big DoDods						
MicroDoDods						
Service #1						
Service #2						
Service #3						
Service #4						

You use it to keep track of your progress on each of those lines. At the end of January, it looks like the following:

AJAX

	Relationship with Key People	Understand the Customer's Need (Peeled the Onion)	Presented Our Match	Negotiated the Next Step	Deal!	Follow Up to Leverage Satisfaction
Widgets	✓	✓	✓	✓		
Red Widgets	✓	✓	✓			
Green Widgets	✓					
DoDods	✓					
Big DoDods	✓	✓	✓	✓	✓	✓
MicroDoDods						
Service #1						
Service #2						
Service #3						
Service #4						

At the end of March, it looks like this:

AJAX

	Relationship with Key People	Understand the Customer's Need (Peeled the Onion)	Presented Our Match	Negotiated the Next Step	Deal!	Follow Up to Leverage Satisfaction
Widgets	✓	✓	✓	✓		
Red Widgets	✓	✓	✓			
Green Widgets	✓	✓	✓	✓	✓	✓
DoDods	✓					
Big DoDods	✓	✓	✓	✓	✓	✓
MicroDoDods	✓	✓	✓			
Service #1	✓	✓				
Service #2	✓	✓	✓			
Service #3	✓					
Service #4						

Each month or each week, as you plan for the next series of sales calls, you use it to assess your progress and focus on the next most important step.

You can find other applications for the process concept and the matrix as a tool to implement it. Your process may be different from the Target System I've described. That's fine. The important thing is that you have a well-defined process, and that you use that process as a way of keeping you focused.

As you do, you'll become more organized, more sure of yourself, and more focused on the important outcomes of every sales call. That sharp focus will make you more effective. You'll sell more in less time. You'll make your boss happy and get your life back!

Tips from the troops...

Make "ish" appointments. In other words, instead of making an appointment for 10 a.m., make it for "10-ish." That way, you can be 15 minutes late, or 15 minutes early, and not have that impact your day.

To implement this management secret:

1. Sketch out your sales process. Work with your sales manager to identify a process if your company doesn't have one that it teaches.

2. Create the matrices discussed in this chapter, using the steps in your sales process. Or use the forms in the Sales Management Tool Kit.

3. Use this as a tool to keep focused and organized.

The Ninth Time
Management Secret:

Nurture Helpful
Relationships!

Early into one of my sales positions, my boss informed me that the operations manager was upset with me. I was too task-oriented and focused in my dealing with the company's internal personnel who made things happen in the business. I'd come into the office, drop projects and requests on everyone's desk, and head out again.

My task-oriented behavior was upsetting people. As a result, they were balking at cooperating with me. My projects were being left on the bottom of the pile, and other salespeople were getting more cooperation.

I had better change my attitude, he told me, or I'd find it very difficult to succeed in this organization.

My lack of good relationships with the people who could make things happen for me was hurting my performance. Eventually, I came around to understand that. I swallowed my pride, bought each one a six-pack of premium beer, apologized, and started focusing on building positive relationships with everyone inside the company.

That was a turning point for me. From that point on, I could accomplish far more because I had gained the willing assistance of a number of people. In so doing, I stumbled onto a powerful time management principle: *Creating relationships that result in people gladly working to assist you can be one of your most powerful time management strategies.*

Tips from the troops...

Make note-taking a habit. Be sure you have a functional note-taking system, using yellow pads, daytimers, your laptop, or PDA.

What seems like an obvious conclusion to a lot of people took me a very painful experience to see. I, like so many field salespeople, was accustomed to working pretty much by myself. No one else in the car with me. Most of the time I was alone when I made a sales call. When I was in my home office planning for next week, I was doing that by myself. Most of what I did, I did by myself. So, naturally, when faced with any task, I did it myself. Just like you, and the vast majority of field salespeople.

It is a part of our mindset to think of ourselves as Lone Rangers—masked good guys out there in the field doing battle alone. We don't think about enlisting the aid of other people. That mindset can be a major obstacle in our effective use of time. Here's a poignant example from my experience.

At one point in my career, I was the general manager of a rapidly growing custom-packaging company. The materials manager was a key position in my organization. This person made sure that the hundreds of items we needed for our custom kits were in stock when we needed them. But she had attendance problems, and after months of trying to help her establish good work habits, I had to fire her.

This brought on a crisis. The position was critical and I couldn't go even a day or two without someone performing the task. In my rapidly growing organization, there was no backup for her. So I took over and did her work. After the end of the workday, I'd then stay and work till midnight or so, doing her job of ordering sufficient materials. This went on for a month or so, until I was able to hire and train a replacement.

Later, I met with the president of the company, to whom I reported. As I told him the story, he said to me, "Dave, why didn't you call here and ask for help? We have several people in the home office who could have stepped in temporarily and done her job."

I was stunned. "I never thought of it," I answered. It just never occurred to me to ask for help. The problem was me! My lone ranger salesperson mentality cost me hundreds of hours over those several weeks.

But I'm not unique. Most salespeople have burdened themselves with a similar mentality. That mentality is a major obstacle to overcome.

There is yet another obstacle to implementing this powerful time management principle. Salespeople generally do not have authority. No one reports to them. No assistants, and no secretaries. If you are going to enlist the aid of people around you, you cannot, therefore, just delegate and rely on your management authority to make it happen. You have no management authority. No one has to do what you ask them to.

If you are going to get people to help you, you must influence them to do so willingly. You must sell them on helping you. Which you can do, because, after all, you are a salesperson!

For what tasks can you enlist help?

Almost everything you do, with the exception of meeting face-to-face with your customers, can probably be delegated to someone who can do it better or more efficiently than you can. Here are some of the things that I have passed off to other people in my career. I offer them to you to stimulate your creative thinking about what you may be able to download to someone else.

I'm not talking about computers here. When I say "download" I mean to move a task from your list to someone else's. I don't use the word "delegate" because that implies that the people to whom you are assigning the task have an official reporting relationship with you. That's not the case. If someone takes on one of your tasks, it's generally because they agree to, not because you are their boss and you are telling them to.

◙ **Finding qualified prospects.**
Why should I spend my valuable time searching through lists or driving up and down? I can give my criteria to someone else, and have them do this work for me.

◙ **Calling for appointments.**
You know how frustrating this can be. Leave a voice mail message. Sometimes the person calls back. You're not there, or you are in the middle of a sales call and have your cell phone turned off. You return the call, get voice mail and the cycle repeats. Instead, someone who is at a desk all day can call, leave a voice mail message, and be there when the prospect or customer calls back. Give them a selection of times when you are available and have that person schedule your appointments.

◙ **Mailing information to prospects and customers.**
One 5-minute phone call to enlist the assistance of a helpful customer service rep can save you 30 minutes of finding the right literature, stuffing the envelope, searching through the junk sliding around the backseat of your car for the right address, etc.

◙ **Compiling useful reports.**
My company provided weekly sales reports, showing every item ordered, shipped, and invoiced to every customer. That was nice, but I wanted to see patterns over time. In other words, I wanted to know what they bought this week, last week, the week before that, etc.

So, I had my kids cut up the computer reports, sort them by customer, staple them to scrap paper, and file alphabetically in my account folders. Great bonding experience with the kids. Before I made a sales call, I'd review that compiled information and know what kinds of purchasing patterns my customers were following. That was helpful.

▣ **Reviewing reports and highlighting the useful information.**
Instead of looking at every item on a back order report, I had someone highlight those more than two weeks old. I'd look at only those items. Saved me time. Made them feel important.

▣ **Looking up prices for bids and quotes.**
I could sit on a computer for an hour or so looking up costs for a complex bid, or I could have someone else do it.

▣ **Turning my penciled notes into nice looking bids and quotes.**
This was before I became adept at using templates and a laptop. Now I can do it faster than I can give it to someone else to do. How many words per minute do you type? If you are a hunt-and-peck person, maybe you should consider this one.

▣ **Checking on the status of back orders.**
I could spend hours on the phone, or intent upon my computer screen, or I could rely on my customer service people to provide me specific information by certain times. Which makes more sense to you?

▣ **Expediting back orders.**
Ditto.

▣ **Filing.**
My teenagers needed something to do to earn their allowance. Better them than me.

◙ **Cleaning out the car.**
Ditto.

◙ **Calling customers following delivery to ensure that they received everything.**
That's what those inside salespeople and customer service people are for. It's a nice touch. The customer is impressed that someone cared enough.

◙ **Training customers in new product applications.**
Technical service people, manufacturers' reps, and others can do this while I can be out selling something else.

◙ **Making emergency deliveries.**
Calling a limo service and having them pick something up and deliver it is cheaper than you taking an hour of expensive selling time for this task. Makes a bigger impression, too. You just need to convince your boss.

◙ **Dropping off samples.**
Why should I drive out of the way and take valuable selling time to drop off a sample to a receptionist or receiving department? Surely there's a better way. Taxi? Limo service? Unemployed teenager?

◙ **Taking orders.**
Why should I spend valuable sales time writing down orders, and then calling the office to relay them? The customer can do that. I'm there to talk about their needs and my solutions, not to be a clerk.

This litany of possibilities is designed to stimulate your creative juices. Once you get into the mindset, you can make all kinds of things happen.

Who can you enlist to help?

The world is full of people who can help an overworked and overwhelmed salesperson. Some of them include:

◙ Customer service representatives.

◙ Purchasing and inventory people.

◙ Product managers and marketing personnel.

◙ Operations managers.

◙ Your boss.

◙ Your spouse.

◙ Your kids and family.

◙ Manufacturers' and distributor's representatives.

◙ Your customers.

Continually seek things to download

Every few months, make a detailed list of all the things you do in a typical week. Then look at the list and ask yourself, "Is there anything on this list that could be done by someone else?" Chances are, almost everything on this list could be

---

Tips from the troops...

Use commuting time to dictate letters and notes to yourself. Make use of a handheld recorder.

---

done cheaper or better by someone else. There is a single exception—no one else can create and maintain the relationships with your good customers except you. You are a unique human being, and your relationships are unique to you.

But probably everything else—all the tasks that fill much of your day—could really be done better or cheaper by someone else. Someone else can check up on a back order, develop a price quote, or fill out a RFQ more efficiently than you. Someone else can make a dozen phone calls to prospects more effectively than you.

Could you be more effective if you had someone else do many of those tasks? If you could free yourself from the tasks that could be done more efficiently by someone else, couldn't you then redirect your time in ways that would make you more effective?

The answer, of course, is yes. You could be far more effective if you could so structure your tasks to allow you to spend more time on the high value-producing tasks and less time on the low value producing tasks.

This is as much an issue of mental habits as it is anything else. Because of our Lone Ranger mentality, we rarely even think about the question, "Can I find someone else to do this?" We just jump right into the task. By disciplining yourself to ask that question, you'll find dozens of things to download.

Sell everyone

Maybe sell is too strong a word. What I really mean is create relationships with all the people around you, such that, when you ask, they are inclined to help. You know how to do this, because you create relationships with your customers. Think of all the people around you as customers, too.

Be polite. Take a personal interest in what they are doing and what they are interested in, offer to help them when you can. Be sensitive to the stresses and demands they face in trying to do their jobs. Don't make unreasonable demands. Most people are not waiting patiently for you to dump work on them.

Remember, the people surrounding you, whether it's your boss or your spouse, are on your side. They want you to succeed. A little humility and sensitivity on your part will go a long way. You might be the mighty breadwinner and the superstar, but please and thank you are still important words to memorize.

Download well

Start with, "I need your help." It's amazing what those words can do. They let people know that they are important, because you are asking them personally. It positions you as humble—you can't do this thing without them. If you have done your homework, and have created good relationships with these people, then they would have to be either overworked already, or a miserable jerk not to give your request serious consideration.

Next, explain your situation—why you need help. Don't just say, "Could you look up the prices for these 76 line items?" Instead, say, "I have this quote due tomorrow at Smith Brothers. It came up overnight. If we can get this business, it'll open

---

Tips from the troops...

Ask for your bill when your food is served. This will allow you to get it while you are eating so that you won't have to wait for it.

---

the door to that account, and I'm sure we can leverage that business into more. I'm already committed to be at Jones Manufacturing this afternoon, so I don't have time to do it. Could you please look up the prices for these 76 line items?"

You've asked for help, you've explained why. Now, wait for a response and then lay out the specifics. So, you've just asked Bill, one of the CSRs to help. Bill says, "I'm right in the middle of this project, but I should be done in an hour. I can do it for you then."

You reply, "Thanks, Bill, I really appreciate it. Here's a list of the items. They are numbered from one to 76. If you could just create a spreadsheet and list the prices in the order in which I have them, and then email that to me so I can work on it tonight, that would be great. Thanks again."

Notice that you now have laid out the specifics, giving Bill an exact understanding of what the task is, and a deadline for completion.

Let's review the process:

1. Ask for help.

2. Explain your situation.

3. After their response, give them the specifics— exactly what and when.

Use this process with people with whom you have created positive relationships—you know them, are interested in them, sensitive to them, concerned about them—and you'll be able to download major parts of your job, freeing up time for face-to-face selling. And that's where you make your money and provide value to your company.

Nurturing relationships with the people around you, and then downloading tasks effectively will help you take your time management skills to a new level, rendering you both effective and efficient.

To implement this management secret:

1. Make a list of all the tasks that you could conceivably download to other people.

2. Make a list of all the people around you who could conceivably help you.

3. Brush up your relationships with them.

4. Identify the combination of tasks and people that you think holds the greatest potential for improving your effectiveness and efficiency.

5. Implement the download process:

   - Ask for help.

   - Explain the situation.

   - After they say yes, show them the specifics.

(Use our salesperson's downloader to help you through this process. It's in the time management tool kit.)

The Tenth Time Management Secret:

Stay Balanced!

P icture the way a sailboat operates. Its majestic sails catch the wind and power the boat forward. But if a sailboat were only equipped with sails, it would be impossible to steer. It would be blown aimlessly across the water, continuously responding to the constantly shifting direction and velocity of the wind. In order to be manageable, a sailboat needs, deep beneath the bottom of its hull, a keel. A keel is the heavy appendage that extends deep into the water and holds the sailboat down. You may remember the year that the United States lost the America's Cup race for the first time in more than 100 years. The culprit? The notorious winged keel on the Australian boat. It was the keel, not the sails that made the difference.

A sailboat with a keel and no sails will sit motionless in the water. On the other hand, a sailboat with sails and no keel will blow whichever way the wind pushes it. It's the dynamic tension created by those two opposing forces—that which powers it in response to the wind and that which holds it back—that provides the sailboat the ability to be directed no matter what the course and character of the winds. The secret to its power lies in the balance between the two opposing forces. A perfectly balanced sailboat, where the two opposing forces precisely complement each other, is a sailboat operating at its peak.

So it is in the life of a salesperson. In order to make the most effective use of time, a salesperson has to stay in balance— perfectly positioned in the dynamic tension between opposing life forces.

The sails in the life of a salesperson are those things that speed you up, that accelerate your growth and your success, that energize you and empower you. The keels are those things that hold you down, that fasten you to ideas and people, that limit your behavior and reduce your choices.

If you are going to be an effective time manager, you need to balance the driving forces with the limiting forces in your life. You need to live within the zone of dynamic tension between those two pressures so that you can be your most effective all the time.

Think about it. If you are not as effective as you could be, you are wasting a good deal of your time. Even one sales call made when you are not at your best could be a waste of time. Remember that smart time management has far more to do with effectiveness than efficiency.

If you are in balance, you are working at your highest level of effectiveness. Staying in balance keeps you at your best, day in and day out, week in and week out, monthly, yearly, for the long term. A sailboat coursing along in the zone between the two forces is one that is operating as close to perfect as possible. It's an experience of beauty, a thrill that requires almost no effort on the part of the sailor.

Tips from the troops...

Before you leave in the morning, make sure that you have a list of the nearby prospects—potential customers that are near the location where you have appointments. If one of your appointments cancels at the last minute, you may be able to use the time to make a prospecting call.

So, too, is a salesperson sailing ahead at the intersection of opposing forces. An effortless zone. Living in balance is the ultimate effectiveness strategy. It allows you to be at your peak most of the time, and that means that you are operating at maximum effectiveness.

Life sails for the salesperson

What are some of the sails you need to first build into your life, and then to continually trim and adjust?

▣ An acceptance of personal responsibility.

▣ A propensity to take risks.

▣ An attitude of openness.

An acceptance of personal responsibility

It is amazing how liberating a real sense of personal responsibility can be. It's also amazing how few people really experience it.

It's far more popular to be a victim. We have all shook our heads sadly over a newspaper story about someone who commits some act of irresponsibility, and then successfully sues someone else for millions of dollars. In our litigious world, being a victim often pays. That is an unfortunate consequence of an unhealthy belief.

As long as we view ourselves as victims, we're unable to change our circumstances and achieve better results. It is not our fault that we're not doing better, we tell ourselves. Someone else caused it. And because it's someone else's doing, the power to fix it and make it better is with someone else. We're powerless to fix it.

While few people admit it, or even realize it consciously, this victim attitude is very common, and embraced to some degree by most of us. This is especially true of salespeople, who could always do better if only something were different—something that someone else controls. If only we had lower prices...our quality was better...the boss was more understanding...customer service was more responsive. You know the litany because you've chanted it.

My wife is a crisis counselor. One of the biggest eye-openers for her occurred when she realized that she was counseling the same people over and over again. You'd think, as she did, that a crisis would be an isolated event. Not so. Many of her clients find themselves lurching from one crisis to another. Why? Because they don't make the changes in their behavior and character that got them into the crises in the first place. At some deep level, they see themselves as victims, not personally responsible for their own character, their own behavior, and the consequences that behavior brings.

A few years ago we visited the country of Albania, just after the communist government fell. We stayed in a government villa close to the main square in the capital city of Tirana. In the morning, our driver would show up and we'd go off for the day's events. We'd pass the square and see thousands of people milling around. In the evening, on our way back to the villa, we'd repeat the experience. After a couple of days, we noticed that the same people were there in the morning and the afternoon, day after day.

When we asked the driver what they were doing, he replied, "Nothing. They are just waiting around for someone to tell them what to do."

A generation of repressive, dictatorial government had robbed the population of the ability to think for themselves, to assume personal responsibility for their situation.

I had a personal experience that brought this lesson home to me in a way that I will never forget. I had been the number-one salesperson in the nation for a company—my first full-time professional sales job. I had it made: adequate salary, good benefits, company car, bonus potential, and the respect of my employer and colleagues. But the opportunities were limited, and I decided to move onto a job that was 180 degrees different. That's when I took the position selling surgical staplers to hospitals. It was a huge leap from the secure job I had to one that paid straight commission, required you to buy your own samples and literature from the company, and provided only six months of a draw to begin.

But I was cocky, filled with the success of my previous job, and sure that I could make this work also. I wasn't hasty. I looked at the amount of existing business in the territory I was slated to get, and determined that if I could double the business within six months, I'd be making close to what I was accustomed to. Then, as I increased the business, my income and lifestyle would illustrate the difference.

It all sounded good. I left my old job and arrived in New York City for six weeks of intensive training on the new one. During the time that I was there, my district manager moved on and was replaced. When I arrived home after the training, the new manager was anxious to meet with me. In our first meeting, before I had a chance to begin working, he informed me that he had revised the sales territories. The territory that I thought I had—the one I was hired for—was not the one I was going to get. Instead, I was going to receive just a fraction of that.

The new territory only contained about one-third of the existing business of the previous one. This change meant my plans for making a living were shot. It now became an impossible task.

I was upset and angry. How could they do that to me? I had five kids to support. I immediately began to look for another job, determined to quickly leave this unethical, uncaring company.

Things got worse. As I interviewed with several companies, I discovered that they saw me as the problem. Instead of understanding what the company had done to me, they thought I was an opportunist who was looking for an easy way out. It became clear that no one else was going to hire me!

I grew more and more angry and bitter. In addition, I had little success selling the staplers. After six months, my temporary draw came to an end. I owed the company $10,000, was making almost no money, and had no prospects for another job. I felt squeezed between the proverbial rock and hard place. I was a victim of a dirty deal.

Then, out of the blue one day, I had a revelation. *It was me!* The problem was *me!* Yes, the company had treated me poorly. Yes, they had been unethical and uncaring. But the product was still exciting, and the opportunity still great. The real problem was my attitude—my bitterness and anger were getting in the way of everything.

I was responsible for my own behavior, my own thoughts, and my own attitude. When I realized that it was me, I felt like 1,000 pounds had been lifted from my shoulders. If the problem was me, then I could change! If the problem was somebody else, then I was a victim, and powerless to do anything about it. What a motivational and exhilarating realization!

I began to work on my attitude. I began to take control of my thoughts. I looked up Bible verses that were very inspiring. Verses like, "If God is for you, who can be against you?" "If you have faith like a mustard seed…." I wrote them down on 3 x 5 cards. Then, as I drove into my territory every day along I-96 in Detroit, I held them in my hand on the steering wheel, and read them over and over to myself. Slowly I began to do away with my bitter attitude, and replace it with hope and expectation.

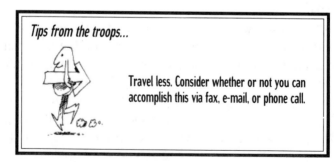

Tips from the troops…

Travel less. Consider whether or not you can accomplish this via fax, e-mail, or phone call.

My results began to change also. Things began to go better. Six months later, I had paid off the debt to the company, and was making more money than I thought was possible. The job became more fun, more financially rewarding, and more fulfilling then anything I ever expected.

The changing point occurred when I realized it was me, not them, who was at fault. It was my personal responsibility to change.

The acceptance of personal responsibility is a sail, powering energy and success for all of us.

A propensity to take risks

Don't get the wrong idea. We're not talking about skydiving here. Nor are we talking about sinking your life savings in the new start-up dot-com that your neighbor told you about. I don't mean taking risks that might endanger your health, safety, or long-term security.

Instead, I am talking about taking risks that force you to move out of your comfort zones on the job—risks that will stimulate you to stretch yourself, to become more competent, to gain skills that you may not have, to expand your abilities and maybe, help you become more effective and more efficient.

When I began my business, my focus was 100 percent on consulting. I had never given a seminar in my life. But I read the books on how to build a consulting practice, and all the experts recommended giving seminars as a way to build a consulting practice. I was determined to do so. I developed a program— How to Find, Interview, Select and Hire a Good Salesperson— and approached the local business college with a proposal to jointly present it. They agreed, and a few months later, I presented my first seminar. It was a huge risk—something I had never done before. It caused me to stretch myself and to learn a new set of skills. The seminar was successful and led to another, and to more. Within a couple of years, I had realized that speaking and training could be major parts of my practice. Today, my speaking and training income exceeds my consulting income by a great distance.

If I hadn't taken that first risk, I would never have built a speaking practice and traveled all over the world presenting. Not only has my income expanded, but my life has broadened, and I've gained new skills.

That's the kind of risk I'm talking about. If you can build a propensity to take risks into your job, you'll grow faster and go farther than if you remain safely inside of your comfort zones.

You take risks in a lot of ways. When you call on a different type of customer than that with which you are comfortable, you take a risk. For example, when you call on the chief financial officer of a business instead of just the production supervisor, you've stepped out of your comfort zone and taken a risk.

When you choose to implement a new strategy or tactic, like rearranging your territory to invest more intensely in your A accounts, you take a risk. When you choose to try a new way to make a presentation, build relationships, or handle objections, you are taking a risk.

Some of those risks will turn out well, others will become failures. Regardless, you'll become more competent, more confident, and more effective. That's what good time management is all about.

An attitude of openness

You don't learn anything from people who agree totally with you. You only solidify and harden your beliefs. It's for this reason that every cult and manipulative organization or person seeks first to exclude their followers from communicating with people who think differently.

I once worked with an extremely manipulative minister who sought to control the loyalty of his followers by influencing them not to talk with people who thought differently. He did that by planting seeds of doubt and distrust. "Be careful about talking to that person; he'll spread rumors about you." Or, "So and so is having trouble in her marriage, so don't talk with her because you're liable to push her off the deep end." All of these cleverly planted seeds of doubt served to prevent communication that could have caused people to learn and change their thinking.

When I was a child growing up, the religious institution in which my parents raised us taught that it was sinful to visit a church of another type. We were taught to be afraid to do so. Take even one step inside, and we would somehow be corrupted. That's what we were taught, anyway. I suspect that the real reason was to discourage us from other ideas. We might be challenged to question some of the beliefs we were being taught, if we exposed ourselves to different ideas.

Whether it's a manipulative individual, or a fearful institution, the basic instinct is to cut off people from other ideas in any way that they can. When you do so, you cause them to harden their beliefs, and prevent them from questioning and growing.

The opposite tactic, then, becomes a means of enhancing your growth. If you want to grow, improve, and become more successful, then you need to expose yourself to people, practices, and ideas that are different from your own. You need to nurture an attitude of openness.

Add these sails to your life, and watch yourself gain speed and power. Then, put them in juxtaposition with the keels that slow you down. That's when you begin to perform at your peak.

Life keels for the salesperson

The keels in the life of a salesperson are those things that give you substance, that hold you back and tie you down.

In order to stay on course, in order to be effective, use time wisely, and stay afloat in all kinds of conditions, salespeople need to build keels, as well as sails, into their lives. They need those things that provide them depth as well as energy. They need direction as well as power.

Some keels are:

- An examined spirituality.

- A chosen character.

- A set of higher ethics.

An examined spirituality

What's a section on spirituality doing in a book about time management for salespeople? I believe it's the starting point for a transformation to greater success in your life and your job. It's at the very heart of who you are. When you make changes in your spiritual beliefs, those beliefs shape everything that you do. Your spiritual beliefs shape your worldview and your worldview determines how you see everything in your life.

Years ago, my wife and I visited Soweto, a large African township that is part of the greater Johannesburg, South Africa metroplex. At the time we visited, some of the children in the elementary school were skipping school in a sort of loosely organized strike. From our perspective, that was pretty unusual. Even more unusual, however, was the reason for this strike. They were objecting to being graded as individuals. In their tribal culture, either the whole class passed or the whole class failed. To separate one child out of the group as doing better or worse than another was to attack a deeply held, spiritual belief about how they saw the world and themselves. They saw themselves less as individuals and more as members of a group.

Think about how that worldview will impact the lives of those children for as long as they live. This was a deeply held spiritual belief underlying their culture, probably below the level of conscious choice, which will determine much of the course of their lives.

While that may be a dramatic example, the principle applies to all of us. Our deeply held spiritual beliefs impact everything we do.

Yet, few people ever examine their spiritual beliefs. The beliefs that are handed down to them are good enough for them. They never examine whether those beliefs are right or true. They only hold on with emotional attachments to beliefs held mindlessly.

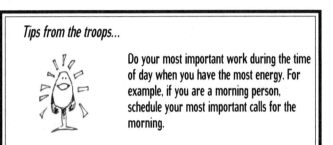

Tips from the troops...

Do your most important work during the time of day when you have the most energy. For example, if you are a morning person, schedule your most important calls for the morning.

I am writing this in the aftermath of September 11. It occurs to me that the actions of the terrorists are a powerful example of an unexamined spirituality dictating the course of their lives. People can so deeply believe things that they lose all touch with reality, and that which is good becomes bad and that which is bad becomes, in their mind, good. I wonder if the terrorists have ever stopped to examine their spirituality—to question the core beliefs and to ask if these are right and true. What if they are wrong? What if murdering innocent men, women, and children isn't a good thing commanded by God? What if they have been deceived by a belief system that is fraudulent?

Have you ever examined your spiritual beliefs? Have you held them up to the light of what is reasonable? Have you considered what evidence there is for you to believe what you do?

If you have examined your beliefs to the point where you are convinced that they stand up under the light of critical inquiry, then you can move on, secure in knowing that you have shored up and supported that most basic and deep part of yourself.

A continuously refined character

It wasn't so long ago that we had political elections in which one of the much-bantered about phrases was, "character doesn't count." The idea behind that cliché was that if a person does a popular job in his political office, his personal character was a non-issue.

What garbage! Not only does character count, but character is probably the single most important component of a successful life.

Here's how Webster's defines character: *an individual's pattern of behavior or personality; moral constitution.* It's our pattern, the way we can be counted on to act and react. When faced with a possible confrontation, some of us can be counted on to become aggressive, others reasonable. Some may avoid the confrontation. At this point in our lives, our pattern is pretty much set, and we can be counted on to act in that way. In other words, how we generally act in certain situations is a predictable pattern for most of us. It's part of our character.

Our character determines, more than anything else, our destiny. For every action there is a reaction. Every time we do something, we cause some response or reaction in other people, or we influence the course of some events. So, if we routinely respond to confrontation by becoming aggressive, that aggression prompts other people to resist us. Instead of having a pattern of cooperation, we create an expectation of resistance around us. And that leads to people making decisions about us that are not in our favor.

Wonder why you didn't get that promotion you were expecting? It probably had more to do with your character than anything else. Can't figure out why that customer went with the competitor, when you knew you had a better solution? Maybe it was you, not your offer.

See how this works? People react to your character—your pattern of behavior. And the way people react to you determines, to a large degree, how successful you are going to be in your life and in this job.

Your character is the composite of the ingrained habits you have created over the years. Many of these habits have become so deeply embedded that you don't even think about them, you just do them.

A habit is created when you repeat an action enough times that it becomes an unconscious pattern. The very first time, as a young child, that you chose to respond to a confrontational situation didn't create a pattern. But by the time you repeated that action a number of times, you established a pattern that became part of your character. It was repeated actions that turned into habits. Those habits became your character. Your character determines, to a large measure, your success.

We can take our analysis of how this works to one more very significant level. At some point, the stimulus to our actions—those same actions that eventually became crystallized into our character—began with our thoughts. Before we can do anything, we must first think it. Remember learning to drive a car? You had to think about every step of the process, from fastening your seat belt to turning the ignition switch to stopping at a red light and so on. You had to think the thought before you could do the deed. Then, after thinking about it over and over again, it became an unconscious habit. But the starting point was a thought—a conscious, willful decision to do some action. Our character, then, is the ultimate result of our thoughts.

Let's review this cause–effect sequence. The way we influence people and events determines our success in life. That pattern of behavior that determines how we influence people and events is called our character. Our character is the assemblage of habits that we have created over the years. Our habits are the results of our repeated actions. Our actions began with our thoughts.

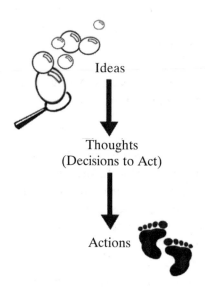

Ideas

Thoughts
(Decisions to Act)

Actions

Here's an incredible principle, certainly one of the most powerful laws in the universe:

> ## You can change your thoughts!

That's right. You can choose to think the kind of thoughts that you want. And when you choose your thoughts, you change your actions. When you change your actions, you modify your habits. When you modify your habits, you shape your character. When you shape your character, you control how you influence people and events. When you influence people and events, you shape your success and your destiny in this life.

This is one of the most powerful truths in the world. And like all such truths, wise men have discovered and rediscovered it from time immemorial. Two thousand years ago, the Apostle Paul wrote, "Be transformed by the renewing of your mind."

Paul meant that you can transform yourself—your character and the way the world reacts to you—by renewing your mind, by changing the way in which you think.

More recently, Martin Seligman, Ph.D., in the book *Learned Optimism*, described how you can choose to think about adversity in your life, and how that choice of thoughts impacts your level of optimism or pessimism, and how that determines the degree of success you have in your life.

This should come as no surprise to the wise student of human behavior. Of course, your thoughts determine your actions, your actions set your habits, your habits become your character, and your character influences your destiny.

If you can choose your thoughts, you can, therefore, refine your character. Bill Gothard, the great Bible teacher, holds that there are 49 character traits that we choose over the course of our lives. We choose for example, to be generous or stingy; courageous or cowardly; responsible or irresponsible.

Sooner or later, the serious pursuit of the effective use of time comes up against this truth. Over the long term, it is not the tactics you employ to be more efficient that determine your success, it is the character that you exhibit. It is more who you are than any techniques you employ.

The long term challenge, then, for you, is to become a person of continuously refined character—a person who has chosen your thoughts, and shaped your character to become the kind of person who positively influences events and people around you.

A set of higher ethics

There are some ethics that are particularly important for a performance-conscience salesperson. These include honesty, integrity, a serious work ethic, and a genuine concern for other people. Let's consider each.

Honesty and integrity

Honesty can be defined as telling the truth. The dictionary defines integrity as: *intactness, firmness of character*. It means that you are who you portray yourself to be—that your habits and commitments can be counted on. You're not changeable and fickle.

These are of great value because they stimulate trust in your customers, and trust saves you time. I was speaking to a group of professional salespeople in Johannesburg, South Africa, on the subject of integrity in business. At dinner later in the evening, my host, who had been sitting in the audience, sheepishly shared with me that several of the people seated near her snickered at the idea. Evidently, to them sales was just a series of transactions, and the salesperson's job was to wring as much money out of each transaction as possible, under whatever means were necessary.

Their position was, I believe, sad as well as unwise. Honesty is a powerful sales strategy that is probably more important today than ever before.

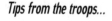
Tips from the troops...

Improve your reading skills. Take a speed-reading course; it will save you hundreds of hours each year.

It works like this. If you have integrity, you save your customer time. In today's frenzied world, time is more precious than money for a lot of people. If your customers cannot believe you, then they must spend hours, days, or weeks of precious time confirming the representations you have made. If, however, they can believe you, then they don't feel the need to check for the veracity of every fact or statement.

Here's an illustration. A few years ago, we attempted to purchase a condominium in a suburb of Cape Town, South Africa. The condo was in a resort location, and had been used as a rental unit. So it came fully furnished, down to the silverware and cooking utensils. We thought it was a good value, a wise investment, and, offered the owner exactly his asking price. Shortly thereafter, word came from the real estate agent that the owner, on receiving our full-price offer, had increased his price.

The owner may have been looking at his action as a slick negotiating ploy. We saw it as a lack of integrity. If we couldn't believe his stated price, then we couldn't believe any of the representations he had made. We would be reduced to counting the number of knives and forks instead of believing the inventory sheet provided for us. We didn't want to waste the time checking out every aspect of the deal. If we couldn't trust some of the representations by the owner, then we couldn't trust any. If we couldn't trust any, it wasn't worth it to us to take the risk in dealing with him. We walked away from the deal.

We saw the owner's lack of integrity as causing us to invest a great deal of time to assure ourselves that the risk was worth the money.

The same is true of your customers. The more your customer trusts you, the less risk your customer feels in dealing with you, and the less time necessary to invest in understanding the product, service, or program you are offering. From the customer's perspective, it's easier and less risky to deal with someone you trust than with someone you don't.

And that can translate directly into dollars. I'm always willing to pay more for something if I can buy it with less risk. In other words, if I can buy it from a company or person I can trust. On the other hand, I'd rather not buy something at all if I have suspicious feelings about the vendor.

A serious work ethic

One of the reasons that I've been successful is that I've always worked hard. I learned that value from my parents. It's one of those ethics that people respect and that will serve you well over time. Notice I didn't say work a lot. The average field salesperson in this country works about 49 hours a week. While there are some temporary situations that may call for you to work more than that, I'm definitely not recommending that you do. Working hard doesn't mean that you work more hours than others. It does mean, however, that you focus on giving those hours your absolute best.

Think about your job in the way that I described in Management Secret Two. You fearlessly and relentlessly pursue your goals and strategies. You follow your company's directions and do what they ask you to do. You don't take 30-minute coffee breaks three times a day and long, leisurely lunches. You work hard. You give it your best. You use every minute as if it may be the only one you have.

Tips from the troops...

Use coffee breaks to write thank-you notes, return phone calls, and read the news.

And as a result, good things happen to you. Every so often I run into a salesperson who has a story of some good thing that just fell on him. It seemed to come out of the blue.

I always congratulate the salesperson, and then inquire into the specifics of the good fortune. It can almost always be traced to some work that salesperson did somewhere in the past. It just took a while to come to fruition. I've found that the luckiest salespeople, coincidentally, happen to be the hardest workers.

A genuine concern for other people

There is something in human beings that hungers to be understood. There is something that wants others to care about us. These human appetites well up out of the deepest parts of our psyche. All of us want people to care about us and to understand us.

Your customers do, too. Of course we're focusing on business issues and the business environment. Still, it is impossible to divorce these powerful hungers from our business lives. And that goes for your customers, too. It's not just about price and product, it is about feeling understood, about feeling that someone really truly cares about us. When your customers feel that you truly do care about them, then they trust you more, share more with you, and buy from you.

This sense that you care about your customers is an incredibly powerful component in the customer–seller relationship. It is tough to fake, although some people do. To be believable long term, it has to be genuine. That means that you need to develop the value of really truly caring about your customers.

In balance

Blending those things that hold you back and limit your behavior with those things that speed your growth and empower your efforts brings you into peak performance. Emphasize sails without keels and you're likely to dissipate hurricanes of time furiously going nowhere. Emphasize keels without sails and you're likely to be stuck in an unmovable rut where nothing changes, especially you. When you build solid keels into your life and juxtapose them with powerful sails, you live in that area of dynamic tension between these two opposing forces that brings out the best in you. You become that which you are capable of becoming, you move out of the world of working hard into the area of working smart and becoming more effective.

Living in balance is one of the greatest time management strategies.

To implement this management secret:

1. Analyze yourself in light of the sails discussed in this chapter. Try to determine, as objectively as possible, to what degree you exhibit each of the sails (or use our Sails Assessment in the Tool Kit).

    - A sense of personal responsibility.

    - A propensity to take risks.

    - An attitude of openness.

    You may want to have someone close to you (a spouse, good friend, or your boss) do the same for you.

2. Develop a plan for stretching yourself in each of these areas. Focus on action. For example, if you find yourself lacking in a propensity to take risks, identify some risk that you could take that would stretch you in this area. Do the same with any of the three areas that need expansion.

3. Repeat the process above with the keels.

Index

A

B

C

About the Author

Dave Kahle is a consultant and educator who brings a unique combination of experience and skills to his clients. He speaks with real-world experience, having been the number-one salesperson in the nation for two different companies in two distinct industries. He combines that with a deep understanding of how people learn best. As a result, he creates seminars and educational products that stimulate people to think and change people's lives.

He's helped thousands of salespeople improve their performance, spoken in 39 states and six countries, published more than 400 articles, and has had his books translated into four languages and sold in 20 countries.

For additional resources on time management, visit *www.salestimemanagement.com*.

For information about the author, visit *www.davekahle.com*.